Your Towns and Cities in the Great War

Wakefield
in the Great War

Tim Lynch

Pen & Sword
MILITARY

First published in Great Britain in 2017 by
PEN & SWORD MILITARY
An imprint of
Pen & Sword Books Ltd
47 Church Street
Barnsley
South Yorkshire
S70 2AS

Copyright © Tim Lynch, 2017

ISBN 978-1-47384-741-5

Typeset by Concept, Huddersfield, West Yorkshire HD4 5JL.
Printed and bound in England by CPI Group (UK) Ltd,
Croydon CR0 4YY.

Pen & Sword Books Ltd incorporates the imprints of Pen & Sword Archaeology, Atlas, Aviation, Battleground, Discovery, Family History, History, Maritime, Military, Naval, Politics, Railways, Select, Social History, Transport, True Crime, and Claymore Press, Frontline Books, Leo Cooper, Praetorian Press, Remember When, Seaforth Publishing and Wharncliffe.

For a complete list of Pen & Sword titles please contact
PEN & SWORD BOOKS LIMITED
47 Church Street, Barnsley, South Yorkshire, S70 2AS, England
E-mail: enquiries@pen-and-sword.co.uk
Website: www.pen-and-sword.co.uk

Contents

Acknowledgements

This book owes a huge debt to the memory of Kate Taylor MBE, a passionate historian and prolific writer on Wakefield's history and heritage. Kate had begun work on researching the city's part in the Great War but was taken before she could begin writing her planned book. I was fortunate enough to inherit some of her material from the publisher. I hope my own research and this finished product would meet with her approval.

Like all authors, Kate gathered material from a wide range of sources and like all historians knew that material well enough to have a catalogue in her mind of what came from where. Where possible I have acknowledged pictures and quotes from her work but the possibility of error on my part means that if I have failed to properly credit anything given to Kate I sincerely apologize and will ensure that any mistakes are corrected in future editions. Likewise the photographs used in this book are credited where the owner is known. Most come from my own collection and are taken from sources where they were originally not credited or where the original owners cannot be traced. No breach of copyright is intended and if information is received, proper acknowledgement will be made in future editions.

I'd like to thank Roni Wilkinson at Pen & Sword for offering me the chance to write about Wakefield. Having worked in the city on and off for many years I've come to have a great affection for it. Thanks too, to Brian Elliott for editing my deathless prose.

As ever, huge thanks to Jacqui, Beth and Josh for leaving me to mutter to myself over the laptop in the corner of the room and for the top ups of wine, coffee and chocolate without which the publishing industry would be a barren place. Although he's from Keighley, my dad, Albert, can be a mine of information about the interwar years and some obscure references to long gone products and practices – the 1930s are clear but last week can sometimes be a bit hazy!

CHAPTER 1

The Last Summer

On the morning of 28 June 1914, Archduke Franz Ferdinand, heir to the throne of the Austro-Hungarian Empire and his wife, Sophie, left the Town Hall in the Bosnian city of Sarajevo in a motorcade heading for the city's hospital. Earlier that morning, after two of his comrades had decided not to go through with their plan to assassinate the pair, a third man had thrown a bomb at Ferdinand's borrowed touring car. The device skidded across the roof, fell into the road and exploded as the following vehicle drove over it, wounding the passengers and at least sixteen of the bystanders lining the route. The Archduke had calmly carried on with the planned visit to the Town Hall, reading his speech from notes spattered with the blood of a wounded aide, but afterwards asked for a change to the itinerary so that he could go to visit the injured in hospital. Mistaken orders to the driver took the car down a wrong turning and directly into the path of 19-year-old Gavrilo Princip, another member of the Serbian group intent on killing Ferdinand as part of the fight for Serbian independence. Hemmed in by the dense crowd, Princip was unable to pull out and prime the bomb he was carrying, so instead he reached for his pistol, but couldn't move enough to actually aim it. As he later explained, 'Where I aimed I do not know... I even turned my head as I shot.' The killer fired just two bullets but at such close range he could hardly miss. One shot hit Sophie in the stomach while the other struck her husband in the neck, severing his jugular vein. There was nothing any doctor could have done to save either of them. Both remained seated upright while being driven to the Governor's residence for medical treatment and Count Harrach, one of Franz Ferdinand's aides, heard him pleading with his dying breath: 'Sophie, Sophie! Don't die! Live for our children!' Sophie was dead on arrival at the Governor's residence. Franz Ferdinand died 10 minutes later.

The murders shocked the diplomatic world but the deaths of one of what a British newspaper called 'Austria's idiot Archdukes' and his

Police arrest one of the conspirators involved in the assassination of Archduke Ferdinand, Sarajevo 1914.

wife in a country far away meant little to the majority of people in Britain, whose main concern at the end of June 1914 was, in keeping with proud British tradition, the weather. A heatwave was gripping the nation, with temperatures hitting ninety degrees in the shade in London, and a record 132 degrees recorded at noon on Wednesday, 1 July. Ten people had been reported dead as a result of heatstroke across the country. The news from Sarajevo was reported but was quickly overshadowed by the events of the afternoon of that Wednesday when, almost as a portent of things to come, the heatwave ended with a devastating explosive thunderstorm. 'The lightning was unusually vivid and almost continuous', reported the *Yorkshire Post*, 'and the thunderclaps came like a series of sharp explosions.' Wakefield itself escaped the worst of it but the torrential rain quickly flooded Bradford city centre and struck parts of Leeds as drains failed to cope with the sheer volume of water. Near Pontefract, farmer Henry Harrison was killed by lightning and 17-year-old Ernest Rhodes was struck at Carlton. In Castleford, miner Isaac Barnes was reported to have been temporarily blinded by a nearby strike.

As the weather became more settled, events abroad as the European powers edged closer to war, took up an increasing amount of space in the papers, but it still seemed remote and few thought Britain would need to become involved. Of more immediate concern was that Wakefield's population had already long passed the 50,000 needed for it to apply for Borough status, making it independent of the West Riding County Council, but they opposed granting it and the matter was being hotly debated in Parliament and in the Yorkshire press. The Wakefield councillors argued that they needed greater powers to address local problems and, like other rapidly expanding industrial towns, issues around health and housing were rapidly becoming a serious concern. In 1910, one in five babies in Wakefield died before its first birthday, a rate twice the national average, with children of unskilled workers being twice as likely to die as those of the professional classes. The 200 deaths per 1,000 births in Wakefield contrasted sharply with 105 per 1,000 nationally, and just 60 per 1,000 in the London Borough of Hampstead. The stark numbers reflected very different living conditions.

The rapid growth of Wakefield and its surrounding districts had seen the population rise from just over 38,000 in 1801 to 193,000 a century later, and to 234,000 on the eve of war. Such a massive rise meant that housing was in short supply and sanitation almost non-existent. To meet demand, John Lee, a Wakefield solicitor, invested in a scheme that built only the shells of back-to-back houses, leaving the purchasers to finish the insides. Buyers looking for properties to rent rarely bothered to make them comfortable, and the result was that developments like those funded by Lee created ready-made slums as large families moved into cramped terraced homes with few, if any, of even the most basic facilities. Writing in 1869, local doctor Netten Radcliffe described housing conditions along Westgate as 'eminently adapted to foster infectious disease', where the cellars of some homes were almost always flooded to a depth of around 6 inches with a mixture of water, sewage and 'liquid refuse from the slaughterhouse nearby'. An 'abominable excrement odour' hung over Spotted Leopard Yard, off Kirkgate, and in one yard a midden shared by several households was built directly under the scullery window of a home. In other places, they were built directly alongside the walls of houses and raw human waste seeped through the walls into family homes, where up to a hundred people shared a few small rooms.

Living conditions in some Wakefield homes were basic and often a danger to health.

Improvements were made but progress was slow. In 1905, the Wakefield medical officer, Thomas Gibson, identified eighty-eight houses as what he called 'the worst of a bad lot' and suggested they be demolished. The Sanitary Committee, he recalled, '... after it had recovered from the shock, decided that fourteen houses should be closed, but nine of the fourteen were eventually re-occupied after some repairs had been carried out.' The Housing and Town Planning Act of 1909 put pressure on local authorities to do something about the worst slums, but for the generation that would go to war in 1914, the damage was already done. In his 1912 Annual Report, the medical officer for nearby Batley provides us with some idea of what such conditions meant for those living in them:

> In all cases where these children died the houses swarmed with flies, the consequence being that their food was quickly polluted. In some cases the Health Visitor reported that the houses were very untidy and the mothers did not trouble to take steps to prevent the pollution of the child's milk although urged to do so ... the outstanding features were artificial feeding and the swarms of flies. In several cases the grandmother gave directions to the mother as to the child's feeding and on more than one occasion

the Health Visitor's report states 'grandmother would not hear of child being breast fed'... A baby living in such a house and artificially fed is really lucky if it survives its first year of life, the probability being that it will succumb to diarrhoea before its first birthday.

In describing one such death, the medical officer recorded:

... one-roomed dwelling occupied by father, mother and three children. Back-to-back house. About a hundred flies in room. Large unpaved yard at side of house, also stable draining onto surface of yard and large heap of horse manure on yard. Several foul privy middens in and adjoining this yard. Rabbits and hens. Altogether the yards are in a bad state, being polluted with filth and excrement of various kinds.

Enteric Fever was another killer easily contracted in the filthy streets:

This child regularly sat in the gutter and played over a street gully down which the residents persistently poured slops and faecal matter although warned not to do so. The child's hands were regularly soiled with faecal matter and he became infected.

Child workers on pit screens. Harsh working conditions, poor diet and bad hygiene meant that when war broke out, thousands were found to be unfit for service.

On average, he reported, a 13-year-old child in these conditions had the physique found in 11-year-olds in more prosperous areas, standing around 2½ inches shorter and 10lbs lighter than their compatriots. Around 60 per cent of schoolchildren had some physical disability linked to malnutrition, 90 per cent had severe dental problems and in some schools headlice infestations ran at 100 per cent. By 1914, remarkable efforts had brought Wakefield's infant mortality rate down to 105 per 1,000 births, but it was still claimed by anti-poverty campaigners throughout the war that a soldier in the front line actually had a better chance of survival than a working-class baby in its cot. In terms of the coming war, a great many would-be volunteers found themselves rejected as physically unfit for military service due to the effects of childhood deprivation.

Unsurprisingly, poorer families looked in anger at the conditions they were expected to tolerate and began to demand improvements.

'Half timers' starting work. Children would spend half their day at work, and the other half at school.

The years leading up to 1914 have been dubbed the period of 'the great unrest', as one industrial action followed another in a nation-wide battle to increase wages and establish better working conditions. In 1908, more days were lost to industrial action than in the whole of the previous decade and the following year a series of strikes severely hit the whole of the crucial coal industry leading the then Home Secretary, Winston Churchill, to order troops into south Wales to restore order among the 30,000 protesting miners of the area. Prime Minister Asquith had made it clear that the government would use all means to control strikers, but plans to mobilise the Territorial Force were vetoed for fear that the Territorials might, as locals themselves, choose to side with their work colleagues and neighbours. Between 1910 and 1914 the number of industrial disputes rocketed, reaching a peak of 872 in 1912, with 40 million days lost to strikes – ten times the total of any previous year. As part of a national dispute, the seaman's strike in Hull saw 500 police officers drafted in from London to control the crowds and restore the peace after rioting began. Matters came to a head in Liverpool on 13 August 1911 as a crowd of 80,000 people marched on the city's St George's Hall. To contain the crowd, local police had been reinforced by officers from other areas and by troops of the Warwickshire Regiment. Fighting broke out with 186 people taken to hospital for treatment and ninety-six arrested, triggering two nights of violence. The Riot Act was read out and more troops were drafted in, supported by a naval gunboat moored in the Mersey. On 15 August, prison vans transporting many of those previously arrested to court and escorted by armed cavalrymen of the 18th Hussars were attacked by a crowd on Vauxhall Road. Bottles and bricks were hurled at the soldiers as rioters tried to grab the reins of their horses. Fearing for their lives, the Hussars opened fire, killing 20-year-old John Sutcliffe and 29-year-old Michael Prendergast and wounding three other men. Since the strikers included railwaymen who supported their fellow workers, the government found it could not move troops around the country to respond to local flare-ups as other areas protested the killings in Liverpool. Four days later – just as the strike was being settled – two more men were killed during more rioting in Llanelli when soldiers facing a hostile mob again opened fire. Across the country, up to 50,000 troops were eventually deployed to maintain order as strike after strike broke out. In Leeds, where armed troops had been deployed to guard the city's railway stations, James O'Grady, Independent Labour Party MP for Leeds

East, urged men not to enlist in the army 'as they are thereby liable to be called out in times of industrial dispute to quell, and possibly shoot down, their fellow workers who are struggling to better their conditions'. Robert Escritt, Independent Labour Party MP and City Councillor for East Leeds joined in with his own call that local men should not 'don the King's uniform, don't take the King's shilling. Until you know that you will not be called upon to shoot your fellow working men, don't join the army.' By the end of 1913, things were looking bleak and the Reverend P.D.Woods wrote in his parish magazine that 'As we look back over 1913 we must all feel that it was a year marked by a spirit of unrest . . . Most of us, I feel sure, will not regret the dawning of 1914.'

Hard though it may have been for Reverend Woods to imagine, the new year showed that things could still get far worse. In January, a military barracks in Leeds housing police and army reinforcements brought in to manage the long running city-wide strike was damaged in a bomb attack using dynamite. Militant suffragettes were involved in small-scale arson and bombings across the country, including one at the pumping station of the Dunford Bridge reservoir, near Barnsley, that reports claimed could have resulted in serious flooding of nearby homes.

Against this background of industrial and civil unrest and domestic terrorism came the real fear of an all-out war on the streets of Britain as tensions between nationalists and loyalists in Ireland escalated and threatened to cross the water. In March, badly phrased orders had led British troops in Ireland to refuse a command to move to protect armouries against loyalist groups if fighting broke out between the two factions, and created a crisis that undermined the British military and political leadership at a tense time in negotiating the future of Irish sovereignty. In April, the Ulster Volunteer Force had openly boasted of landing 25,000 rifles and up to 5 million rounds of ammunition at Larne in readiness for armed action against nationalists seeking an independent Ireland. In response, July saw the Irish Volunteers land 900 rifles at Howth but in marked contrast with the lack of opposition to the Larne operation, the police and army intervened and a gun battle broke out leaving three dead. The same month saw a conference at Buckingham Palace consider the partition of Ireland with all nine counties of Ulster becoming separated from the rest of the country. With a potential civil war on their own doorstep, the people of Britain were distracted from the prospect of war in Europe. Then Germany sided with its Austrian neighbours.

For the last twenty years, the people of Britain had been bombarded with stories of invasion by foreign powers ranging from France and Russia to H.G. Wells' 'Martians' but the prime candidate in over 300 novels alone had been Germany as the country most likely to try to destroy Britain and its empire. In March 1913, an audience at the Wakefield Empire had been addressed by Colonel Hind of the local Territorial battalion who told them that Germany's army was growing and that it had a fleet of thirty Zeppelin airships, each capable of carrying twenty-five men or five tons of explosives. Men were urged to come forward to join the Territorials to protect their homes and families from an invasion that could come at any time. In military displays, films, plays, books and short stories, the people of Britain were warned over and over that an attack by Germany was inevitable and it was only a matter of time before jack-booted soldiers would march on British streets. In one of the best selling invasion novels, William Le Queux's *Invasion of 1910*, a German force landed at Goole and Wakefield was identified as one of their first targets as they overran the industrial heartland of the country. At the turn of the century, German support for the Boers had been seen as part of a wider strategy to undermine the British Empire overseas but its latest activity was seen as direct evidence of its intention to destroy Britain itself – all the weapons landed in Ireland by both sides as the nation teetered on the brink of a civil war that could spill over into England had been supplied to them by Germany.

By 1914, strikes and lockouts were commonplace across the whole country as the ever strengthening unions prepared to take on the government but whilst industrial actions might make life more difficult for ordinary people, they still gained popular support. In late June, 584 men from Wrenthorpe Colliery were summonsed for leaving work to attend a demonstration linked to their ongoing strike against the Low Laithes Colliery Company without giving the required fourteen days notice. On the day of their appearance the men had gathered outside their pit and, led by a brass band and with wives and children in tow, marched together into town to attend court. By the time they reached Wood Street there were thousands of well wishers lining the route and gathered outside the courthouse. After a week's adjournment, on 3 July, each man was fined £3 under the Employer and Workmen Act for losses caused by the walkout. Another 200 men were fined in Ossett for the same offence.

At the end of July, a gruesome discovery was reported when Normanton bricklayer William Stones and three workmates began work on the pump of a well at Park Lodge Farm in Stanley on behalf of new tenants who were moving in. Lifting two large flagstones, Stones climbed down a ladder and found the body of a baby girl floating on a plank. The head and part of the shoulders were missing and the rest of the body badly decomposed. The police were called and, to the surprise of the coroner, Stones reported that having found the body, he had then calmly gone to have his dinner. Giving evidence to the court, Stones described how George Wilcock, the previous tenant, had told them that he saw no reason to 'meddle with the well' and that it was 'a bit of a conceit' that the new owners could not drink water that Wilcock's family had been using for over thirty years. After bringing the body out of the well in a basket, Stones called Wilcock over to see what they had found in his drinking supply. Wilcock seemed unsurprised, but when told the police had been called asked 'why didn't you go and bury it in the field and there would have been nothing more about it?' Police Sergeant Woolley went to the home of Wilcock's daughter, Kate Jewson, at Garden Street in Wakefield, who immediately confessed to having put the child into the well, saying she thought 'it' was dead. A post mortem found a cord around the stump of the neck and the court proceedings were adjourned so the well could be drained in the search for the head. Jewson was later tried for 'concealment of a birth'.

Brighter news came in the last week of peace when the great and the good descended on the area to celebrate the 21st birthday of Rowland George Winn, eldest son of Lord St Oswald, at Nostell Priory. Rowland's birthday, on Wednesday, 29 July, marked the start of a four-day celebration, as men and officials of Frodingham Iron-stone Mines presented him with 'an illuminated address' – a finely carved oak casket contained a book illustrated with drawings linked to his family and life, including pictures of men at work in the family's mines and scenes from around their estates and holdings in Lincolnshire. The villages of Foulby and Wragby were decked with bunting and the terraced colliers houses of Nostell Long Row festooned with flags to welcome Rowland home from his posting with the Coldstream Guards. On the first day of the celebrations members of the Lincolnshire Iron Masters Association along with tradespeople

Rowland Winn, seen here as a cadet.

from Wakefield and Pontefract and tenants and employees of the Nostell estate were all treated to lunch in the grounds. The next day, 1,300 employees of Nostell Colliery were invited for tea and on Friday, another 1,300 employees of the family's Lincolnshire estate were brought by special trains for another celebratory tea. Saturday was reserved for special guests including Russian aristocracy in the form of Count Michael de Torby and his wife, the Countess Nada to celebrate not only Rowland's majority, but also Lord St Oswald's own 58th birthday, with dancing to the music of the band of the Scots Greys. Proposing a toast, family friend Jonathan Shaw explained how he had known the whole family since the present Lord's grand-father and found them all to be 'true gentlemen'; and said, 'Surely with such examples before him the young gentleman ... ought not to go astray'. A year later, though, some began to wonder if he had ...

CHAPTER 2

Your Country Needs You

Meanwhile, in Europe, the crisis continued to deepen. In response to the assassination of Franz Ferdinand, the Austro-Hungarian Empire had humiliated Serbia with demands that could not be met, and finally, on 28 July, they declared war. The next day Russia began to mobilize its forces in support of its Serbian ally. Germany, siding with Austro-Hungary, demanded that the Russians stop and when the Tsar refused, declared war on 1 August. An agreement between Russia and France to try to contain Germany's plans to expand its empire in Europe meant that the French now began to mobilise their forces. A large-scale war on the continent was seemingly inevitable but not really seen as Britain's problem as newspapers began to consider what the immediate future might bring. Coming after years of unrest, *The Worker* of 1 August 1914 felt that war would be an opportunity for class action, telling its readers that 'the war is no concern of the working class and their duty is to take every advantage of such lapses into insanity by the capitalist class'. Elsewhere, others considered how Britain might be kept out of the war and, at a local level, what the impact of a European war might have on business. The *Huddersfield Daily Examiner*'s editorial of 31 July 1914 explained what war might mean to the West Riding:

> True it is that a general Continental war would in the end injure the prosperity of this country by greatly impairing the purchasing power of many countries which are now very good customers for the products of our manufactories. This calculation ... loses some of its effect from the fact that the extra production which immediate demands from France and Germany in case of war between those countries would occasion in many classes of goods, would go far to counterbalance the loss already mentioned. In the first instance, therefore, Britain has no immediate concern in the strife which is taking place or might take place if

Russia, Germany and France should be drawn into the struggle
... Therefore Britain may continue to work for peace without
any suspicion of selfish or improperly interested motives.

So, although Europe teetered on the brink of war, the people of
Wakefield prepared for their Bank Holiday weekend more or less as
normal. The Wakefield City Tradesmen's Association was preparing
for its annual fete to be held in Wakefield Park on Bank Holiday
Monday, 3 August. The band of the Irish Guards would play
throughout the day from the bandstand at the top of the hill and
there would be a display of that most obvious of holiday entertain-
ments – bayonet fighting while contrasting the military theme would
be a troupe of pierrot clowns and an evening firework display. For
those able to afford a holiday away, the Midland Railway Company
was offering deals on excursions to Yarmouth and Lowestoft, the
south coast and the Isle of Wight, or to south Wales. Some could
look even further afield as the choir of St Helen's Church, Sandal,
set out for a holiday in Belgium on the day that Germany declared
war on Russia, travelling from Hull to Zeebrugge to begin a tour
which was designed to take them to Blankenberghe, Bruges, Haeyat
and Brussels. Even as the choir arrived in Belgium, though, Wakefield
became aware of the imminence of war on Sunday, 2 August, when,
in an unprecedented event, paper-boys ran through the streets at
7.00am shouting 'War special!' and carrying Sunday editions of the
Yorkshire Post as national newspapers announced that Germany had
declared war on Russia.

As they did every summer, the men of the local territorial forces
had set out for their annual training camp, this year to be based at
Whitby. Alongside the Wakefield-based 4th Battalion of the King's
Own Yorkshire Light Infantry (4 KOYLI) were local men serving
with the Yorkshire Dragoons and the Royal Army Medical Corps
(RAMC) as well as the other units of the West Riding Division. The
camp officially began on 26 July but employers were often reluctant
to allow workers a full two-weeks holiday so many men did not arrive
until Saturday, 1 August, followed in many cases by their families,
who planned to take the opportunity for a week at the seaside whilst
their menfolk camped nearby. Even as they arrived, though, rumours
of mobilization were rife. The Territorials, it was said, were to be used
to guard the docks at Immingham. Others said those wearing the
badge of men who had signed the Imperial Service Obligation had

Territorials returning from summer camp.

agreed to serve outside the UK would be sent to overseas garrisons in far flung reaches of the Empire to relieve the regulars guarding them now. The less excitable expected to be sent back to Wakefield to await events.

As the men gathered, the situation in Europe escalated even further. On Friday, the Kaiser had complained that he no longer had 'any doubt that England, Russia and France have agreed among themselves – knowing that our treaty obligations compel us to support Austria-Hungary – to use the Austro-Serb conflict as a pretext for waging a war of annihilation against us ... Our dilemma over keeping faith with the old and honourable Emperor has been exploited to create a situation which gives England the excuse she has been seeking to annihilate us with a spurious appearance of justice on the pretext that she is helping France and maintaining the well-known Balance of Power in Europe, i.e. playing off all European States for her own benefit against us.'

In an effort to control the threat of German expansion, France and Russia had each agreed a pact to come to the aid of the other if attacked, ensuring that if Germany attempted to invade either country it would be forced to fight wars on two fronts – the Western Front against France and the Eastern Front against Russia. So when, on 1 August, Britain agreed to guarantee French neutrality, which would mean that the war could be limited to the dispute between Austro-Hungary and its German ally on the one hand and Serbia and its Russian support on the other, the Kaiser immediately accepted.

He then ordered German forces to be used against Russia alone, leading his senior commander, General Moltke, to point out that it wasn't possible for Germany to do that, given that the bulk of their forces were already advancing towards Luxembourg and Belgium, as the opening moves of an invasion of France. Their plan had been to invade France first in a knockout attack before the Russians could finish mobilizing their army so that both enemies could be dealt with quickly. Putting a halt on the invasion of France, the Kaiser told Moltke that 'it only remains for Russia to back out, too'. Unfortunately, it was already too late. In Berlin, unaware of the new agreement, German Chancellor Bethmann Hollweg had already announced that Germany had mobilized and had delivered an ultimatum to France ordering it to renounce its alliance with Russia or face a German attack. Reports of the German forces on the borders of Luxembourg and Belgium had led France to begin making its army ready and at 7.00pm on Saturday, 1 August, Germany invaded Luxembourg and declared war on Russia. The extent to which Germany was determined to go to war is evident from the incident in which the German ambassador accidentally gave the Russians both copies of the declaration of war – one which claimed that Russia refused to reply to Germany's ultimatum – and the other that said Russia's replies were unacceptable.

In 1839, Britain had been instrumental in establishing the country of Belgium and had signed a treaty guaranteeing its neutrality – a treaty also signed by Germany and France. Honouring that agreement, the British government announced that if Germany invaded Belgium in violation of international law, Britain would have no choice but to go to war. The British Empire, after all, depended on such treaties to guarantee its control of small countries around the world and allowing the Germans to do whatever they wanted would set a very dangerous precedent. The Germans, unable to believe that the British would carry out their threat, ignored it. On 2 August, the British Cabinet met and recognised that an invasion of Belgium and France was inevitable. This would put German forces on the shores of the English Channel and the German navy in ports that threatened Britain's own national security. In response, they promised that the Royal Navy would protect France's coast from German attack. That day, a German ultimatum was delivered to Belgium requiring free passage through the country for the German army on its way to France. Unsurprisingly, King Albert of Belgium refused. On Sunday, 2 August, congregations in churches and chapels across the country were urged to pray for peace and in London alone 15,000 people attended an anti-war rally in Trafalgar Square with many similar rallies held in other cities throughout the day. Special Sunday editions of newspapers appeared on the streets filled with stories of a naval battle being fought in the North Sea. Facts were hard to come by but the German ultimatums to Russia and France were confirmed and the first signs of British mobilization began.

On 3 August, Germany declared war on France. The *Wakefield Express* later reported that holiday excursions had gone ahead but 'with no zest', and although the City Tradesmen's fete had gone ahead in the park there had been a considerably lower attendance than in previous years. An editorial struck a sombre note when, with remarkable prescience, it declared that the coming war 'would put into the shade everything in the recorded history of the world both in regards to the sacrifice of human lives and the outpouring of treasure'. A War Office telegram had gone out to all railway station-masters: 'Naval Reserves mobilised. Honour warrants, and give every facility for transit'. In Whitby, the Territorials began to break camp and 4 KOYLI reached Wakefield late on Monday before being sent home for the night with orders to return to the Drill Hall in the morning. Clerks were already at work preparing joining instruction letters for men who had not been at the camp.

On 4 August, Germany invaded Belgium. A full-page advert placed by the Neutrality League appeared in the *Yorkshire Post* with an appeal to the population to 'keep your country out of this wicked and stupid war'. Trade unions, the Labour Party and others condemned the 'murderous gang of warmongers responsible for the present European crisis' and 'the efforts that are being made to involve this country in the bloody outrage on humanity' whilst the *Worker* news-paper called openly for any outbreak of war to be the catalyst for revolution against the government. By now it was too late. Even the German Chancellor admitted that the invasions of Belgium and Luxembourg were a violation of international law but claimed Germany was 'in a state of necessity, and necessity knows no law'. Faced with such a flagrant breach of international treaties, at 7.00pm the British Ambassador to Berlin delivered an ultimatum to the

German Secretary of State to the Ministry for Foreign Affairs demanding a commitment by midnight that evening to go no further with Germany's violation of Belgium. Convinced that Britain would not honour its promise to Belgium on what was dismissed as merely 'a scrap of paper', Germany assumed the risk of war with a powerful European nation would force Britain to back down. It was wrong. At midnight German time, 11.00pm in Britain, the ultimatum expired and war was declared.

Coming at the end of a Bank Holiday Monday when many thousands had spent a good part of the day in pubs, cheering crowds gathered but there were many reactions to the outbreak of war. Michael Macdonagh, parliamentary correspondent for *The Times*, later described having passed through Trafalgar Square on the evening of the 4th, where 'I found two rival demonstrations in progress under Nelson's Pillar – on one side of the plinth for war, and on the other against!' As the deadline approached, he joined a crowd outside Buckingham Palace as they waited:

> No-one came out of 10 Downing Street. No statement was made. There was no public proclamation that we were at war by a herald to the sound of trumpets and the beating of drums. [After hearing Big Ben strike 11.00pm.] The great crowd rapidly dispersed in all directions, most of them running to get home quickly, and as they ran they cried aloud rather hysterically 'War!' 'War!' 'War!' They were eager, no doubt, to spread the dread news ...

Halifax MP James Parker noted that:

> London is back in the [celebratory] mood, and the blood lust has gripped its people. I hope the provincial towns are meeting the crisis in a far more serious mood. I wish I could blot from my memory the scenes of the last three days. They have been of the kind that shakes one's faith in all those things that make for moral and spiritual advancement in mankind ... I confess I was appalled at the light hearted wrecklessness [sic] of my fellow men and women. Judging by the demonstrations of the crowd it might have been a picnic the nation was entering upon instead of the greatest crisis of a century – shouting, singing, cheering mobs; besides themselves with blood lust and war intoxication. They shouted patriotic songs, sang 'Rule Britannia' they

Crowds gather outside Buckingham Palace after news broke of the outbreak of war.

clamoured onto the tops of the buses, waved miniature Union Jacks and generally conducted themselves in a way that proved they could have no idea of the gravity of the situation. I cannot blame them too much, however, for inside the House of Commons there was a recklessness and enthusiasm for the war that

was horrible to witness … I feel sure my constituents will understand my position. I hate and loathe war; I believe we might have
been kept out of it … The days that are coming will try men's
souls. I beg of all my fellow townsmen to do their best to meet
the sorrow and suffering that is bound to come …

Wakefield woke to its first day at war with a mixture of excitement
and dread. 'On Tuesday', reported the *Wakefield Express* of 8 August,
'the streets presented an unusually busy appearance as the men
passed along carrying their rifles and kit to the Headquarters'. The
Territorials, formed to act as a home defence force for use only in
case of an attack on mainland Britain, were expecting to prepare to
repel a possible invasion. Reporting with them were men of the
Reserves – former regular soldiers who had left the army but were
still eligible to be recalled in an emergency. Most would collect their
papers and kit and head off to rejoin their old regiments so as soldiers
of 4 KOYLI reported to the Drill Hall, clerks were busy dealing with
processing those men as quickly as possible to make room for the
Territorials. The task was made more urgent by the order to the
Territorials to 'recruit to wartime strength and double'. The idea was
that as each Territorial battalion reached full strength, a duplicate
would begin to form. The 4th KOYLI would therefore become two
battalions, those trained and ready would form the first (1/4th) and
the rest would train as part of the second (2/4th) and would initially
act as a reinforcement unit, sending trained replacements to the 1/4th
as needed but later would form a unit in their own right. When 1/4th
went to 49th (West Riding) Division, 2/4th would go to 62nd (West
Riding) Division, with 49th reaching France in 1915 and 62nd in
early 1917.

   Since the Territorials usually went home after training, there was
little space available at the Drill Hall for them to stay until a decision
was made about what they would be asked to do. For the time being,
Companies of 4 KOYLI made up of men drawn from Normanton
and Ossett were billeted in the Town Hall and the Court House whilst
the Dewsbury Company were housed in the newly-built Mines
Rescue Station in Ings Road. The Dragoons managed to find more
comfortable billets at the Bull Hotel, the White Horse, and York
House and the RAMC lodged at St Mary's School. With everyone
eager for news about what would happen next, a reporter from the
Wakefield Express was despatched to the Battalion's headquarters to

find out but was sent packing after the battalion's Sergeant Major responded to his questions by bellowing in full parade ground mode: 'I KNOW NOTHING!' On Thursday, after inspections to ensure every man had his full equipment in good order, the Battalion set out on a route march to Crigglestone during which seventy men dropped out and were declared unfit for service, their places taken by recalled reservists.

The process of mobilizing Britain's army was further complicated by the fact that many policemen, postal workers and railwaymen – those most closely involved in ensuring that recall notices and travel warrants were available – were themselves reservists and were also being recalled. At the same time the West Riding County Council was anxious not to deter men from enlisting so staff who were members of the Territorials left their positions at County Hall and their heads of department were advised that they must not replace them with men who were able to enlist in the forces. To add to the confusion, the *Wakefield Express* reported that the recruiting office in Bank Street was being kept busy with young men who 'seemed prepared to forfeit anything' if only they could enlist. They, too, needed warrants and transport to reach the regimental depot of the KOYLI and the York and Lancaster Regiment at Pontefract where new battalions were being formed from the flood of applicants already coming forward.

In peacetime, the British army could not afford things that would become vital in the event of war. It relied on horse-drawn transport for everything from artillery to ambulances and the delivery of all its supplies in the field but for generations had simply hired wagons and drivers recruited from local civilians as and when it needed them. The system that had worked so well in India and Africa would not work in France, where both horses and drivers had already been drawn into the French army. Now, the army needed to find transport as a matter of urgency. Military personnel from the Remount Service worked with veterinary surgeons to scour the Wakefield area for horses that could be requisitioned, buying fifty of them immediately. Horsepower of a different kind was also being sought and Hebblethwaite's, in Pincheon Street, gave notice that owing to the war and the government requiring the services of motor transport at short notice, all its charabanc excursions would be cancelled from 9 August.

With little or no official reporting, newspapers were keen to pick up on stories about local people returning from Europe. Two Wakefield pork butchers, John H. Kilburn, who had a shop in Kirkgate, and

Requisitioned transport for the Wakefield-based 4th Battalion of the King's Own Yorkshire Light Infantry.

John E. Spurr, whose shop was in Westmorland Street, were with a party from the St Helen's Choir and gave an account of their adventurous journey home to the *Wakefield Express*. When they first reached Belgium, they had not seen any news of how quickly the European crisis had escalated and had been completely surprised by the welcome they began to receive from the Belgians. Everywhere they saw soldiers in the streets with bayonets fixed. In Antwerp they came across German cafes and shops that had been ransacked and saw a convoy of around 250 cars carrying Red Cross nurses towards the front lines. In Dinant they had been ordered off a bridge because it was about to be blown up. Once they understood the seriousness of the situation, they attempted to return to England as quickly as possible but had found it impossible to get a ferry back from Zeebrugge and had to go on to Ostend, finally reaching Wakefield, via Folkestone, on Friday, 7 August. By 21 August, newspapers as far afield as Dundee and Dublin were expressing fears for the safety of the Moorhouse and Pickering families who had settled in the Alsace region of France, but were originally from Wakefield. Both were reported to have spinning mill businesses in Haguenau, and Jesse Moorhouse was described as having lived in the area for over thirty years. They still maintained their connection with Jesse's son, Harry, representing Green & Co., a Wakefield firm manufacturing fuel economisers in Alsace-Lorraine, and his daughter had married a German and was living nearby in the town of Colmar. With the whole family fluent in French and German, the *Yorkshire Evening Post* was able to confidently tell its readers on 21 August that there was 'not much cause for alarm' in respect of either family.

Among the luxuries a peacetime army could not afford were the military hospitals it would need to treat the wounded in time of war. When the part-time soldiers of the various old Militia, Yeomanry and Volunteer units were amalgamated into a single Territorial Force in 1908, it had been realised that if ever they were actually needed for the home defence duties against invasion for which they had been created, no provision had been made for their health care. So poor was the army's medical support that during the Boer War of 1899–1902, civilian volunteers from the St John Ambulance Brigade were sent out on six-month tours of duty to act as field medics and in the years following, even the regular army could muster just 300 nurses worldwide to treat its sick and injured.

To try to rectify the problem, the Territorial and Reserve Forces Act of 1907 made provision for medical and nursing support by creating the Territorial Force Nursing Service in 1908, along with the Queen Alexandra's Imperial Military Nursing Service Reserve as a back up in times of emergency. The plan was to create twenty-three regional territorial force hospitals in towns and cities throughout the country, each with planned accommodation for 520 patients and a staff of ninety-one trained nurses drafted in to run them. However, they would exist only on paper until war broke out. In the event of war, the plan was that schools and other public buildings would be requisitioned and everything from beds to bandages would be sourced from the local community. With little support from hospital authorities who discouraged their nurses from joining the Territorial Force and training limited to just seven days every two years for those ranked as Matrons, it was clear that even staffing these hospitals would be a major problem, let alone the problems associated with establishing them. It is a measure of the efforts that the nurses made that by the end of August 1914, nineteen hospitals were up and running with the remaining four operational by mid-September.

Recognising the difficulties facing the Territorial Force Nursing Service, on 16 August 1909 the War Office issued its 'Scheme for the

Organisation of Voluntary Aid in England and Wales,' which laid out an agreement with the Red Cross and St John Ambulance Brigade to set up both male and female 'Voluntary Aid Detachments' to fill certain gaps in the Territorial medical services in England and Wales, with a similar scheme for Scotland following in December of that year. By early 1914, there were 1,757 female Voluntary Aid Detachments (VADs) across the country and, although nowadays usually associated only with women, another 519 male VAD units were registered with the War Office.

Wakefield had been quick to respond to the call and, under the enthusiastic leadership of Lady Catherine Milnes Gaskell, of Thornes House, Mrs Barton (the wife of the headmaster of Wakefield's Queen Elizabeth Grammar School) and Mrs Nellie King (headteacher at Clarendon Street Girls School), the 31st (St John's Wakefield) VAD was the first to be formed in the north of the country. The female detachments varied in size according to local conditions, but in the main consisted of a commandant, a medical officer, a quartermaster, and twenty-two women, two of whom were supposed to be trained nurses, but by 1914, Wakefield had sixty-four volunteers attending their regular training sessions. VADs were required to meet at least once a month, with many meeting as often as weekly, and the women had to work towards gaining certificates in Home Nursing and First Aid within twelve months of joining. They were taught how to apply bandages, to do simple dressings and the basics of invalid cookery and hygiene. In some areas it was arranged for them to go into local hospitals for a few hours each week to gain an insight into ward work, and as a result of the low number of men being recruited in certain places, women could also gain experience in outdoor activities, stretcher duties, the transport of sick and wounded and improvisation of transport for the wounded with whatever came to hand. Some didn't take their responsibilities too seriously, while others were intent on being well-prepared for a role that they might never be called upon to fulfil. The volunteers were intended for home service only as a way of staffing auxiliary hospitals and rest stations and they received no payment or salary for these duties – all the women had to be in a position to give their services for free so membership tended to be drawn from the wealthier families.

As the Territorials of the KOYLI prepared for their annual camp, Lady Catherine, already in her fifties and with a long record of seemingly indefatigable community work, led her VADs to the grounds of

Calder Farm Reformatory in Mirfield, where tents and marquees had been set up to create a field hospital, and over the weekend of 25–26 July the Wakefield VAD was put through its paces by Sergeant Jagger of the Wakefield company of the Royal Army Medical Corps Territorials. After a 6.00am reveille on Sunday they were guided through the tasks they would be expected to carry out in actual warfare before attending worship in the Reformatory chapel. Later, they were told fierce fighting had taken place nearby and were sent out to search for and collect the 'wounded' within a radius of 3 miles; and to take them to a notional collecting hospital using commandeered farm wagons as their ambulances, and the female volunteers joined them at the 'hospital' to assist the medical orderlies. Within days, it seemed, they might be needed for real.

When war broke out, plans to convert Clarendon Street School into a hospital for the wounded were considered but were soon abandoned and the disappointed pupils returned as normal at the end of the summer holiday. It was also suggested that the newly built West Riding police headquarters in Back Bond Street (now Laburnum Road) might be converted into a hospital, but, again, for now, there was no need. The Wakefield Board of Guardians, who held responsibility for the dependent poor and for the Union Workhouse in Park Lodge Lane, already had plans to extend its own infirmary to provide 200 beds rather than the existing 148, and at its first meeting following the declaration of war, members agreed unanimously that thirty-four beds could be made available for the treatment of wounded local soldiers. At the start it was unclear whether or not the VAD should mobilize and an advertisement in the *Wakefield Express* on 8 August advised members to hold themselves ready for service just in case. The same notice asked for donations of equipment, so that if necessary a local hospital could be set up quickly, and in particular asked for single iron bedsteads, mattresses, sheets, blankets, pillow-cases, men's nightshirts and pyjamas, woollen socks, flannel shirts and money. Shops advertised the necessary fabrics for volunteers and women members of the VAD held daily sewing and knitting sessions, making shirts, socks and other items. They also turned to making preparations for the comfort of the soldiers by bottling rhubarb, plums and pears, making chutney and drying lavender to freshen sheets. Pupils at St Michael's Girls School made a dozen pillow-cases and seven bolster cases, paying for the material themselves as the Town Hall became a collecting base for the donations pouring in.

Also being mobilized were the members of the local scouts and guides groups. With so many postal employees being recalled to their regiments, scouts and guides were drafted in to act as messengers (in London, the security service MI5 recruited its own troop of Girl Guide messengers after finding the girls' 'methods of getting into mischief were on the whole less distressing' than those of the Scouts initially recruited). Advertisements soon appeared offering the service of boys and girls for a wide variety of tasks, as clerks, runners, helping to bring in the harvest or any other jobs that might be needed. Others were deployed to guard specific 'vulnerable points' against potential sabotage by the German spies that were believed to have set up large networks to undermine the country from the inside. So important was their work that the wearing of a Scout uniform by anyone who was not an active member of the organisation soon became a criminal offence and some older Scouts proudly wore their uniforms to work.

A scout certificate, c.1914. Scouts quickly became recognised as an official 'public service' after undertaking a wide variety of jobs to help the war effort.

Like most towns, Wakefield also had its own chapter of the para-military 'League of Frontiersmen', an eccentric group of what can only be described as grown up boy scouts later described by Colonel H.R. Pownall as 'mostly, but not entirely, men of middle age – or older, who have "Knocked about" a good deal and like the glamour of a Stetson hat, boots and breeches, and a revolver holster, who, to their great credit, wish to have a useful function in emergency but are of too independent a spirit to stomach the bonds of army discipline in peace.' Formed in 1904 by former Northwest Mounted Policeman and Boer War veteran Roger Pocock, the organization was founded as a field intelligence corps to act as 'the eyes and ears of the Empire' and fears of a German invasion had encouraged a sizeable unit in Wakefield. At the start of the war, the League offered its services to send members behind German lines but were told their services would not be required, although a few Manchester-based men made their way to Belgium as the 'British Colonial Horse'. Later, a battalion of the Royal Fusiliers was formed around a detachment of around 300 Frontiersmen and saw service in East Africa. At home, Frontiersmen came close to being adopted by the security services but in the end the organisation settled for fund-raising and charitable activities instead.

For Wakefield people not in some kind of uniform, the outbreak of war brought more immediate concerns than the risk of attack,

Wakefield's League of Frontiersmen on a charabanc outing.

with the main worry in the first few days of August not the war itself, but the impact it would have on business. Both the *Yorkshire Post* and the *Yorkshire Evening News* of 6 August considered Bradford – virtually a single industry town with Germany as its biggest export customer – to be facing imminent ruin, leading historian A.J.P. Taylor's pragmatic grandfather to observe, 'can't they see as every time they kill a German they kills a customer?' Trade with Germany was particularly important to E. Green & Sons of Calder Vale Road, makers of fuel economisers who had company representatives based in Germany and concerns grew for their safety. Some of the local collieries were dependent on exporting their coal but all shipments from Hull, Goole and Immingham were stopped because of the enormous insurance premiums demanded now the country was at war. Walton Colliery was closed temporarily and it was feared that other pits would also have to close. Joseph Rhodes & Sons, at Grove Iron Works in Kirkgate, had an extensive export business to the continent and a depot at Asnieres, near Paris. By the end of August it had reached an agreement allowing the French government to take over the metal-forming machines that it had there. It was thought that they would be used for making shell cases.

It was not only the export trade that would suffer. Within two days the effects of the war were being 'seriously felt in the majority of trades in Leeds', according to the *Yorkshire Evening News*, adding that similar problems were being reported across the West Riding. Pre-existing plans had put the railways under government control immediately war was declared and now priority went to military transport, leaving civilian freight at depots and unable to move. With no way to move stock, many businesses went on to short working and some were forced to close altogether. Elsewhere, workers met with employers and agreed cuts to wages in an effort to keep companies afloat. The *Wakefield Express* even warned that paper would soon be in short supply as its manufacture was dependent on pulp shipped from Norway and Sweden and the North Sea had now become a battleground. The holiday trade, reliant on income generated over the summer months, abruptly found its livelihood threatened. The Post Office had lost so many staff that mail deliveries were seriously disrupted, again affecting businesses and the requisitioning of horses and vehicles caused severe problems for all types of transport. It was not all bad news, though. Although the *Express* predicted that the worsted and cloth mills would be hard hit, excited manufacturers looked forward to receiving government orders for cloth to make uniforms with Colbeck Brothers & Co. at Alverthorpe, expecting to be working flat out to meet orders for serge and khaki, although ironically the dye used to make khaki had previously been imported from Germany and other sources were now needed, leaving many new recruits starting their military career proudly wearing surplus blue post office uniforms. By early January 1915, Mr. R. Tonge, Secretary of the Ossett Chamber of Commerce, was able to report to the Annual General Meeting that the town was experiencing the greatest boom it had ever known, a sentiment echoed in many mill towns regenerated by government contracts.

Within the first week, though, the situation seemed far more bleak and the immediate impact of war on trade meant that thousands of military-age men found themselves suddenly out of work. Unemployment rose sharply across the country, almost doubling from a pre-war average of 3.5 per cent to a high of 6.2 per cent in August before falling again to 5.4 per cent in September and 4.2 per cent in October, but still remained a serious problem. Early in August, Wakefield Council began looking for schemes to provide work and planned projects to strengthen the foundations of Dewsbury Road, make improvements to Sugar Lane and to widen parts of Barnsley Road, Castle Road, and Flanshaw Lane. Meanwhile, a letter from the West Riding Rivers Board urged the Council to implement sewerage and sewage-disposal schemes in an attempt to alleviate the worst effects of unemployment. As it had for generations before, the army offered some the only alternative to hunger and in some places the Poor Law Guardians simply stopped any support for able-bodied men, advising them to join up immediately. There was concern that the spate of voluntary work in garment-making for example, might aggravate the unemployment situation and pleas were made for people not to undertake work for free that could be done as paid employment. If hospitals were to be established, it was argued, the work of fitting them out should be done by local firms, not by VAD volunteers.

In response to the emergency, on 8 August the *Wakefield Express* carried a letter from the Prince of Wales announcing the establishment of his National Relief Fund to assist both the families of soldiers and sailors and those thrown out of work by the war, and this was supported by a further letter from Queen Alexandra expressing her own support for the scheme of her 'dear son for the relief of the inevitable distress which must be bravely dealt with in the coming days'. Wakefield's Mayor, John William Saville, took charge of local fundraising and donations came in quickly with most of the money being forwarded to the national fund, but part was retained for the relief of local distress. Concerts were organized at the Grand Electric Cinema in support of the appeal and the Playhouse, already helping the VAD, put on additional shows in an effort to help. Employees of the Diamond Coal Cutting Company decided to give up 5 per cent of their wages to the Prince of Wales Fund and to let the Mayor have a monthly payment whilst workers of the Lancashire and Yorkshire Railway gave up 1.25 per cent of their wages for the War Relief Fund. Within a fortnight of war being declared, Wakefield people had subscribed £205 to support the Voluntary Aid Detachment and £2,445 for the National Relief Fund with a house-to-house collection at the end of August by staff from the Prudential Insurance Company, bringing in a further £135. Wakefield already had a Citizens Guild of Help which had been founded in 1910 as a voluntary organization supported by subscriptions to provide immediate assistance to those in financial distress from its premises in Almshouse Lane. For ease of management of the fund, Wakefield had been divided into districts each with its own dedicated team who would investigate every application for aid. As soon as members realised that the War Relief Fund would be fulfilling the same role, the Guild offered their premises and volunteers to manage the payments.

Unemployment was not the only financial concern. Many local miners had already been members of the Territorials, with five of the ambulance men from the West Riding Colliery at Altofts leaving to serve with the Royal Army Medical Corps and around 150 men from Henry Briggs Son and Company's collieries at Whitwood, among those who had immediately been embodied into the KOYLI. For the miners, though, leaving for the army was a serious matter given that army pay of a shilling a day meant an enormous pay cut that few could afford. The local branch of the Soldiers and Sailors Families Association advised those who were dependants of serving soldiers, sailors and ambulance men to register for assistance if required at the office of the National Relief Fund in the Town Hall but having to apply for charitable handouts in order to serve their country did not sit well with the men. Like many employers, Briggs encouraged other men to enlist by promising to give the wives of any employees willing to enlist 10s a week with a further 2s a week for each child while they were away. Low Laithes Colliery Company, operating at Wrenthorpe

and Gawber, and with forty-eight men already embodied, were prepared to provide 10s a week to the wives of servicemen but asked
their employees to support the children themselves. At Newmarket
Colliery the union branch devised a scheme where miners still at work
would contribute to a fund to give 5s a week to the wives of those who
joined up and an additional 2s-6d for each child whilst the owners
of the Victoria Coal and Coke Company at Park Hill Colliery and
St John's Colliery at Normanton offered £3 to every man who joined
up plus 5s a week saved for him until his return. Wakefield Council
followed suit, promising all fifty-two employees already planning to
enlist that their jobs would be kept open for them.

Britain had gone to war with a small, highly professional army but
the newly appointed Secretary of State for War, Field Marshal
Herbert Kitchener, immediately recognised that the army that had
coped well against third world adversaries across the world was now
facing a large, well equipped European enemy. If Britain were to play
any significant role, it would need to expand and quickly. Recruiting
began for the first 100,000 men of what would become known as

Volunteers swear allegiance before being given the King's shilling. The first step to
becoming a soldier.

the 'New Army' or, as the serving troops called it, 'Kitchener's Mob'. On 15 August, Saville's appeal appeared in the *Wakefield Express,* reminding readers of the city's excellent track record in supplying volunteers for the army in time of need:

> As Mayor and Chief Magistrate of the City, I appeal to eligible men to respond to the call of the King in this hour of national trial.
>
> In the year 1900 when the country required Volunteers for South Africa the response from the Wakefield district was remarkable and at the King's Own Yorkshire Light Infantry supplied more Volunteers than any other battalion in England.
>
> In the fateful emergency that now confronts our Empire the need is manifestly greater. MEN OF WAKEFIELD! AGAIN LEAD THE WAY!
>
> The appeal is to both old soldiers and new men. The terms of service are as follows:
> 1. General service for 3 years or until the end of the war;
> 2. Age for old soldiers 19–42. Age for recruits 19–30;
> 3. The families of married men who join will receive separation allowance.

This was followed by the first of several recruitment rallies as crowds filled Wood Street to hear Colonel Christopher R.I. Brooke, who was to head Kitchener's newly formed 8th Battalion of the Kings Own Yorkshire Light Infantry, and Major Simpson, who was in overall charge of army recruitment in Yorkshire, address them from the balcony of the Town Hall. Immediately, 146 men volunteered with more coming forward in the following week. So successful was it that a second and more ambitious rally was held a week later. This time a screen was rigged up outside the Court House onto which were projected lantern slides of admirals and generals. The principal speaker this time was George William Coventry, Viscount Deerhurst, a veteran of the wars in South Africa and Matabele, who was followed by the Yorkshire cricketer-turned soldier, Francis Stanley Jackson, now a Colonel in the West Yorkshire Regiment, and lastly by Wakefield's Liberal Member of Parliament, Arthur Marshall. A week later, the *Sheffield Independent* reported 'exceedingly lively' recruiting at Wakefield, with 900 men accepted for service, 600 of them from that single rally. In a widely reported speech to a recruiting drive near Barnsley, former Admiral Lord Charles Beresford told a

A shortage of uniforms meant that new recruits began training still wearing civilian clothes and often commuted to training from home.

large crowd that 'a pair of Yorkshire eyes behind a British bayonet – they cannot stand bayonets you know – will put more fear into the hearts of the Germans than anything else. Roll on all you lads who can and I wish you good luck. Cheer up Yorkshire!'

Despite the initial enthusiasm, especially from those who would not be joining themselves, across the country the fact remained that only a very small portion of the men eligible to enlist had done so. News from France in late August and early September that the British Expeditionary Force was in full retreat sent recruitment figures soaring to a high of 462,901, but within weeks, the number had fallen to less than a third of that and would continue to fall for the rest of the war. Some chose not to join because only a year earlier the army had been deployed on to the streets during strikes and were still seen as the enemy. Others could simply not afford the loss of income enlisting would bring. Still more saw that after the initial blow to business, the clothing, engineering and munitions manufacturers were bouncing back and there were ample jobs for all. For some, it was pure prejudice. In class conscious Edwardian society the ordinary British 'Tommy' was still regarded with suspicion and as late as 1913 soldiers in uniform had been regularly barred from theatres and music halls. Recognising that many potential recruits were put off by the idea of serving alongside the 'wrong sort', Kitchener's 'New Army' created a new sort of battalion. Following a scheme developed by Lord Derby, battalions would be formed of 'Pals', men from similar backgrounds who would serve in special units where social standards could be maintained. Among the first questions asked of an applicant to the Leeds Pals, for example, was to ask what his father did for a living, and only those from the University and the professional classes would be accepted. So stringent could these rules be that Hull had to create separate battalions for its commercial sector, tradesmen and sportsmen, before allowing ordinary recruits into a ragtag battalion known as 't'others'. In many cases these special battalions were raised and funded by the local council until they could be handed over to the War Office as a fully formed unit. In Wakefield, attempts to have the recruiters for the Leeds Pals visit the town failed, so J. Charles McGrath, Clerk to the West Riding County Council, suggested in early September the formation of a Heavy Woollen District Battalion made up of professional men with 'educational advantages' such as those working for the County or Borough Councils, as businessmen or as clerks in some other sphere. By late September it had become clear that there was little hope of raising the estimated £7,000 needed to clothe the unit, let alone the money needed to train it, and so by mid-October the first batch of his volunteers went to the Earl of Yarborough's estate at Brocklesby House, near Immingham, to join the Lincolnshire Chums instead.

Raising a local battalion was an expensive business. Among the groups attempting to raise their own battalion were the West Yorkshire Coal Owners Association (WYCOA), who put aside £22,000 for the purpose and began recruiting at pits across Yorkshire, but struggled to find enough men willing to join what was already being referred to as the 'Pontefract Battalion'. Many miners had already enlisted but many more fell foul of the new regulations raising the minimum height requirement from 5ft 2ins to 5ft 6ins. Given the difficulties, the WYCOA considered simply donating £10,000 to the War Office instead, but when they approached them, the War Office agreed to waive the rules and to draft in extra numbers from among the other KOYLI volunteers, provided they would be treated the

Early volunteers for Kitchener's 'New Army'.

same as their former miner comrades. It also offered to provide £7-5s per man for equipment and 2s a day for food. Thus encouraged, the WYCOA went back to recruiting what was now being referred to as the 12th (Service) Battalion (Yorkshire Miner's) of the King's Own Yorkshire Light Infantry or, more simply, 12 KOYLI. On Monday, 14 September, 250 new recruits formed up outside the Town Hall and were wished God-speed by the Deputy Mayor before marching through crowded streets to the station to catch the train to the KOYLI depot at Pontefract, their final destination as yet unknown.

Following a request by the Mayor, a rally at Wakefield's Empire Theatre on a Sunday evening towards the end of October was organised by representatives of Wakefield Labour Party, Wakefield Socialist Party and the Trades Council, with the principal speeches coming from leading trades unionists. John H. Thomas, the Member of Parliament for Derby, was the Secretary of the National Union of Railwaymen – the largest trades union in the country at the time – who referred to the possible impropriety of holding such a gathering on a Sunday, but argued that the country had never before been engaged in 'so righteous a cause', adding that it was neither a party issue nor a government issue, but rather one for the whole nation. J.W. Burrows from Wakefield Trades Council then proposed a two-part motion calling on those eligible to volunteer at once for military service and for the government to improve the pay and make adequate provision for dependants. It was seconded by Councillor Tennant who reminded the gathering that the navy needed men too.

The rallies at the Town Hall had urged men to support their King and country and presented enlisting as a patriotic duty. That, though, was not how miners' leaders saw it. For them it was a fight for democracy and freedom of speech. Lofthouse miner Harry Robinson initiated a scheme to persuade young single mine workers to enlist and called a meeting of delegates from other local collieries at New-market Silkstone, Park Hill, Robin Hood and Wrenthorpe, in the Dolphin Hotel. There they organised a rally at Outwood, to be held on 8 November. Initially the plan was to hold it in the school but the crowds were so large that it had to be held outside, with speakers Herbert Smith, the President of the Yorkshire Miners Association, and county councillor and Assistant Secretary Sam Roebuck stand-ing on a hastily rigged platform. Roebuck spoke about how well miners were suited for work on the front line and that they 'made the finest fighting material that could be produced because they lived face to face with exceptional danger every minute of their working life'. Harry Robinson argued that young miners had the stamina to endure the rigours of army training and would not contract rheumatism and have to be sent home. He then repeated the proposed two-part motion calling upon those eligible to enlist at once and for the gov-ernment to increase the allowances for those who were serving, their dependants and to the wounded. It was seconded by a local school-master.

Miners' leaders then arranged a further recruitment rally, again on a Sunday, on the evening of 28 November at the Wakefield Empire. This time there was a large platform party including both the new mayor and his predecessor, three Members of Parliament, including Wakefield's own Arthur Marshall and the Labour members Charles Duncan, MP for Barrow in Furness and secretary of the Workers' Union, and Fred Hall, a former treasurer of the Yorkshire Miners Association, who was the Member of Parliament for Normanton. F. White from Park Hill Colliery proposed another motion similar to the ones at the October meeting and the one at Outwood but specify-

ing £1 a week as the amount the government should pay those whose
soldiers became permanently disabled or the widows of those who
died for their country. Hall, who seconded the motion, stressed the
threat of invasion, referring to the presence of German warships off
the Norfolk coast and a great deal was made about reports of suffer-
ings following the German invasion of Belgium, comments reinforced
by a Belgian soldier by the name of Dubois who was in Wakefield,
briefly, with a group of refugees. The grimness of some speeches was
relieved by the comic turn given by Bryan O'Donnell, mocking the
Kaiser as 'sometimes' mad and the Crown Prince as 'always' mad,
before advising young men that no self-respecting girl would go out
with a lad in a tweed jacket now that khaki was the acceptable colour.

Despite lingering animosity following the struggles of the Great
Unrest, the two leading political parties declared a truce. Thomas
Clayton, the election agent for the Liberals and Tory agent J.T. Mills
wrote a joint letter to the Mayor placing their services at the council's
disposal in whatever sphere they might be needed. Florence Beaumont, the daughter of Herbert Beaumont, a prominent Wakefield
solicitor and Clerk to the Board of Guardians, had been a leading
organiser for the national suffragette movement's pilgrimage from

Protesters from the women's suffrage movement campaigned for the chance to do
their bit.

Newcastle to London and had carried the Suffragette banner as it passed through Wakefield the year before. Now, as Secretary for the Wakefield group, she announced that they were suspending their political activities until the war had ended and that their members were ready to give whatever help was needed to relief committees of whatever kind.

But whilst it seemed everyone was keen to do their bit, for the moment there wasn't really anything for most people to do whilst others were overwhelmed. The barracks at Pontefract were home to two regiments, both of whom were struggling to bring their regular battalions up to strength with recalled reservists whilst at the same time trying to make sure their Territorial Force battalions were prepared. Now they had to cope with a sudden influx of New Army volunteers for battalions that didn't yet exist. As the system broke down under the enormous pressure, men got bored and sought out whatever entertainment could be found, leading to one local citizen to complain that the young men hanging around Pontefract were 'a rowdy lot' compared to the Germans he had seen in Brussels as he made his way home at the start of the war. The comments prompted an angry response from another reader who pointed out that 'it is not easy for thousands of young men to remain sedate in a town which

Newly vaccinated recruits. Many, including medical experts, objected to the practice.

has over twenty licensed premises within 200 yards of the Parish Church' and that they were, on the whole, well behaved.

With nothing much to do and nowhere to entertain themselves when off-duty, bored soldiers began to desert in order to enlist in other regiments where the prospects of action seemed better. Others simply tagged on to drafts of men being sent off to training camps around the country and hoped no-one would notice the extra bodies.

As those who had enlisted waited to begin training, those left behind looked at what they could do. Many young, professional men were in a position where joining up would mean leaving behind family businesses that might not survive without them but at the same time the very real threat of invasion meant they could not sit back and do nothing. Almost overnight, across the country, new groups formed based on the Ulster Volunteer Force that had been created as a citizen's army ready to defend their homes. By December, the Wakefield Athletes Volunteer Force was 120 men strong and began drilling at the Wakefield Rugby Union ground at Thornes and practised rifle shooting at a range provided by E. Green & Sons in Calder Vale Road. Like all such groups, members had to personally pay for their training and equipment and received no help from a government worried about the prospect of an armed citizens' militia on the streets

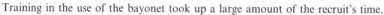

Training in the use of the bayonet took up a large amount of the recruit's time.

of Britain without any central control. Many Belgian civilians had been executed by the Germans and men of the volunteer force would have no protection under the Geneva Convention if the Germans did land, but equally could get under the feet of the Territorial Force who were trained for just such an attack. There were also concerns that joining the volunteers on a part-time basis might be seen by some as an alternative to joining up to fight. Such was the momentum, though, that in 1915, the Volunteer Training Corps was formed as a national body and would remain active even after the Armistice, providing the blueprint for the Second World War's Home Guard.

The Athlete's Volunteers highlighted the major problem facing the country as summer turned to autumn in deciding who should serve and who should stay behind. Men were needed at the front but would be of no use if their equipment wouldn't work as it was meant to. In the rush of enthusiasm back in August and September men had enlisted who were in reality far more use at home and, as the situation settled, some found themselves still in uniform but back at their old jobs. Others considered essential had been told to carry on with their civilian jobs in engineering or munitions but by then the patriotic

With little military training available to them, volunteers take part in a route march.

fervour sweeping the country meant that anyone not in uniform was being targeted as a 'shirker' and sometimes presented with a white feather as a symbol of cowardice by women on the street. Embarrassed by an incident where a man was presented with a white feather shortly after receiving his Victoria Cross at Buckingham Palace, and others where wounded soldiers home on leave were being branded cowards, the government tried to put a stop to the practice but failed. Instead, it began to issue special badges to those employed on essential war work in an effort to try to distinguish between those who were needed and those who simply chose not to go.

The vexed question of who should serve also spilled into the sporting world with a long-running debate about whether professional football should continue in wartime. Some argued it was vital for morale and drew large crowds for the recruiters to work on; others pointed out that footballers who enlisted would be in breach of their contracts and would never play again; still others called for footballers to enlist in order to set an example and lead their fans into the army. The same debate was taking place in other sports, too. Horse racing and fox hunting were both supported on the grounds that the army would need good horses for the cavalry and stablehands enjoyed protected status throughout the war. Cricket was over and players had no real excuse not to enlist. The Yorkshire Rugby Union recommended that play be stopped in the county for the duration of the war but J.B. Cooke, Wakefield Trinity's representative on the Northern Union argued as follows: 'It seems to me far better that the ordinary course be followed rather than the programme abandoned, more especially because of the effect on the public at large. The fact that so many have already volunteered for service is some evidence that the great bulk of players are prepared to do their duty and if others are required they will be in far better trim when wanted if they continue to play the game.' Some players did join up, others didn't. As the season progressed, gate receipts fell and clubs found themselves in financial difficulties. A 25 per cent reduction in wages was ordered by the Northern Union League and soon professional players were threatening a strike. 'Whatever the local opinions as to the players attitudes may be', explained the *Yorkshire Post* of 7 November, '... it is pretty certain that the public at large will not have their dwindling respect for professional football arrested by the present trend of events'. A month later, Wakefield Trinity was forced to call off a match against Hull because of a players' strike, although

THE MUD SLINGERS

The Leader: "Come on, boys, keep it up, some of it's bound to stick."

["The Times" declare that Professional Footballers are shirking their National Duties and that League Matches are a scandal and prevent Recruiting.]

Professional sportsmen found themselves at the centre of a controversy over what they should do, honour their contracts or enlist?

the club seemed less than dismayed: 'As a matter of fact,' one of the Committee told the *Yorkshire Evening Post*, 'the strike has simplified the matter for us. We were running the club at a loss every week. So long as the players remain on strike we shall save that loss. The players are not hurting the club, they are only hurting themselves and if they are well advised they will meet the committee in a friendly way while they still have chance'. It was not an idle threat. Gate receipts had fallen by 50 per cent and most clubs were struggling. A special fund had been set up to assist impoverished players but it was those on the highest wages who complained loudest. By the end of the 1914–15 season, when the decision was taken to stop all competition until the end of the war, 1,500 players in the Northern Union had enlisted, twenty-six of them from Wakefield Trinity.

As a settlement was being reached, everyone involved was given a sharp reminder that there were bigger issues to worry about. On the morning of 16 December, German ships appeared off the North East coast and began bombarding the ports of Hartlepool, Whitby and Scarborough, killing men, women and children, and sparking a panicked evacuation of the towns as civilians fled the invasion many thought had begun. The raid had caused widespread damage, especially in Hartlepool, but it was the shelling of Scarborough that triggered the fiercest response. Known to many as a peaceful holiday destination, 'Remember Scarborough!' became a rallying cry for recruiters everywhere.

By the end of 1914, the war in France had settled into the stalemate that would last until 1918. John Tate from Crigglestone had been among the first to die, killed serving with the Lincolnshire Regiment on 24 August, leaving a widow, Blanche, to collect £2-9s-3d from his unpaid wages. On 26 August, 2 KOYLI were in action and Wakefield men Algernon Cockell, Thomas Gill and William Nottingham were killed. Joe Winrow, also known as Alfred Dyer, was lost somewhere on the road from Mons and presumed dead, his wages paid to his widow, Ann.

With Christmas approaching, Wakefield people tried to find ways to celebrate. There were shortages, true, but the railway companies laid on cheap fares and special excursions so that families could get

Shell damage, Scarborough, December 1914. The attacks on coastal towns became a rallying call for recruiters.

together. Men came home from their training camps and those over-seas received a special gift of tins containing tobacco for smokers or sweets for non-smokers, along with a card and pencil so they could write home. Special funds were set up to ensure no local man was left without something from home to let him know Wakefield was think-ing of him. Under the circumstances, it was a good Christmas.

CHAPTER 3

The Enemy in our Midst

At the turn of the twentieth century Germany was still a very young country but it had already made a lot of enemies. Founded at the palace of Versailles outside Paris at the end of the Franco-Prussian war in 1871, the German Empire brought together no fewer than four kingdoms, six grand duchies, six duchies and seven principalities, along with three independent city ports, all under the overall control of the King of Prussia, Wilhelm I as 'Kaiser' (or Emperor). Wilhelm I ruled a united Germany that stretched from Alsace on the French border deep into the Baltic, covering modern-day Poland, Lithuania, Estonia and eastward to Konigsberg (now Kaliningrad) in what is now Russia. When Kaiser Wilhelm I died in March 1888, his place was taken by Frederick III, who lasted just three months before dying of throat cancer, and the throne passed to his 29-year-old son, who was crowned as Kaiser Wilhelm II in June, and immediately began to make it clear that he intended to rule the empire himself, forcing out his Chancellor, Bismarck, and setting Germany on what he called a 'New Course', which would bring it into conflict with neighbouring countries.

A grandson of Queen Victoria, Wilhelm II was related to several members of European royalty, but was widely regarded by them as arrogant and rude, with one member of his court complaining in 1908 that 'he is a child and will always remain one'. Prone to tantrums and beating or even stabbing servants, even his close friend Count Philipp zu Eulenburg, described him on one occasion as 'pale, ranting wildly, looking restlessly about him and piling lie upon lie, he made such a terrible impression on me that I still cannot get over it'. British Prime Minister Lord Salisbury thought him 'not quite normal' and Foreign Secretary Sir Edward Grey reported he was 'not quite sane'. His relationship with his British relatives were especially bad and he resented what he saw as a lack of respect for his position as Emperor, particularly from his Uncle Bertie, the Prince of Wales. When Britain went

Charles Hagenbach's shop. Swiss born, Hagenbach was spared the abuse that German shopkeepers faced.

to war in South Africa in 1899, Wilhelm openly supported the Boers and in 1905 angered both the French and British by showing support for a growing anti-French movement in Morocco. For the British, who had long regarded themselves as Anglo-Saxons and thus closely related to the German state of Saxony, Wilhelm began to be seen as a growing threat to the Empire and to his European neighbours as he increasingly ignored advice from his political advisors.

The late Victorian era saw an outpouring of books about imagined invasions of England by various foreign armies, with France and Russia as popular potential attackers, but as early as 1871 *The Battle of Dorking* introduced the idea of Germany as an enemy. Written by former army officer George Tomkyns Chesney, it is set in 1921 when a veteran of the war describes to his grandchildren how, in 1871, German troops landed in England and were faced by a British army weakened by spending cuts and unable to resist. It was a theme enthusiastically picked up by others. In 1894, William Le Queux's book *The Great War in England 1897*, described an invasion by French and Russian forces with the weakened British saved by the arrival of German allies but after the political climate changed when Britain agreed an *entente* with France a decade later, his next invasion novel saw a German force landed at Goole. In his 1906 novel *The Invasion of 1910*, Le Queux described how the Germans pushed south towards Doncaster and Sheffield, with barely any resistance:

> The people of the West Riding, and especially the inhabitants of Sheffield, are stupefied that they have received no assistance – not even a reply to the Mayor's telegram. This fact has leaked out, and has caused great dissatisfaction. An enemy is upon us, yet we are in ignorance of what step, if any, the authorities are taking for our protection. There are wild rumours here that the enemy have burned Grimsby, but these are generally discredited, for telegraphic and telephonic communication has been cut off, and at present we are completely isolated. It has been gathered from the invaders that the VIIIth Army Corps of the Germans have landed and seized Hull, but at present this is not confirmed. There is, alas! no communication with the place, therefore, the report may possibly be true. Dewsbury, Huddersfield, Wakefield, and Selby are all intensely excited over the sudden appearance of German soldiers, and were at first inclined to unite to stem their progress. But the German proclamation, showing the

individual peril of any citizen taking arms against the invaders, having been posted everywhere, has held every one scared and in silent inactivity.

Commissioned and promoted by the *Daily Mail*, Le Queux's book proved popular, selling over a million copies and was translated into twenty-seven languages (including a pirated edition published in German). It came among a flood of around 300 such works produced in the decades immediately before the outbreak of war, including H.G. Wells' *The War in the Air* and even *The War of the Worlds*. Alongside invasion literature came stories of German spies such as Robert Erskine Childers' *Riddle of the Sands* and in 1906, the best selling *Boy's Own* paper advised readers that most German tourists in Britain were spies on the basis that they wore jackboots in bad weather, leading an 8-year-old Evelyn Waugh to form a gang dedicated to drilling and preparing for an invasion. In 1909, Guy du Maurier's play *An Englishman's Home*, played to packed audiences with its tale of the takeover of a middle-class house by foreign troops and live performances of staged battles of British forces against 'German' troops were performed at London's Crystal Palace, leaving no-one in any doubt as to what was expected at some point. For many, the supply of German-made Mauser rifles to Irish Republicans in 1914 simply confirmed that the Kaiser was intent on trying to undermine Britain and its empire.

All of which made life uncomfortable for the thousands of immigrants from the German Empire who had settled in Britain over the past half century. Kaiser Wilhelm deeply distrusted Jews, claiming that they had fostered opposition to his rule, and telling friends he believed that they needed to be 'stamped out'. Similar anti-Semitic views in Russia had led to violent riots directed at Jewish families to drive them out of their homes. Thousands had left, many heading for America, but those who could not afford the fare (and some dumped at British ports after being assured they were in New York) reached Britain. A growing anti-immigrant mood grew amongst people in towns and cities, who themselves were often economic migrants from Ireland, Scotland and rural areas of the country.

The British Brothers League and other anti-immigration groups had won a victory in 1905 with the introduction of the Aliens Act which many saw as a defence against Britain becoming 'the dumping ground of Europe', targeting especially refugees fleeing pogroms in

ALIENS IN BRITAIN.

OFFICIAL ADVICE TO GERMANS AND OTHERS.

"Advice to Aliens now in Britain" was yesterday issued by the British Government as below:—

German subjects must all register themselves at the nearest police station. British women who have married Germans have become German citizens, and must be registered. The children of such marriages are in a similar position.

Foreigners desirous to leave will find no difficulty, unless German subjects, if they provide themselves with passports, etc., and make sure beforehand of boat and train services.

No German subject may leave these shores without special permit from the Secretary of State. Males of military age will not be granted such permits. Others must apply in person or through persons representing them (solicitors or others), or in the case of those living at a distance from London by letter to the Secretary, Home Office, Whitehall, London, S.W. Such applications should be supported by documentary evidence as to identification, employment, etc.

Permits are granted only to leave Britain by certain ports and on a given date by a given steamship service. Therefore those applying should make sure of being able to leave a day or two before.

On 15 August 1914 newspapers published notices explaining to foreigners living in Britain what they should do.

Eastern Europe. Although huge numbers of the immigrants were Jews with no reason to be loyal to the Kaiser, that didn't stop the notoriously anti-semitic MP William Joynson-Hicks from assuming the worst:

I do not move my Amendment with any hostility to the Germans in our midst', he told the House of Commons in November 1914. 'For many years England has been the home of foreigners, but I think they should be the first to realise that our first duty is to protect ourselves, and I would rather that irreparable damage should be done to any individual or individuals rather than our country should be placed in danger even for a moment. There are a very large number of aliens registered in this country at the present time. On the 9 September the Home Secretary gave us some figures, and he told us that there were 50,633 alien Germans registered in this country, and 16,014 Austrians. If we were to add ten per cent for non-registration up to that date, then we should get a total of over 73,000 alien enemies. I know it is a very difficult matter to say that A or B is a spy, nor could the Germans or the French say that A or B was a spy before they found him out. I think we are entitled to consider here what happened in the case of France and Belgium. There they have found a complete system of espionage. Soldiers, sailors, policemen, telephonists, tram drivers, professional men of every kind, and men of every class in the working life of France and Belgium have turned out to be spies. Any officer or soldier who has returned from the front will tell you that those countries have been infested with spies. Now England is a greater enemy to Germany than either France or Belgium. The enmity of Germany is more directed against us at the present time and has been for some years past, than against Belgium or France ... On the other hand, England has been the easiest country to enter, and therefore it is fair to assume that as we are considered the greatest enemy of Germany and as ours is the easiest country to enter, we have a larger number of spies than either Belgium or France. You may say that this does not matter unless Germany invades us, but we must prepare for eventualities. Personally, I am not one of those who think that we shall be invaded, but we must prepare for eventualities. If there is no possibility of invasion, why is the Government providing against it? Why are trenches, wire entanglements and other reasonable precautions which sane men would take to protect us being prepared by our military advisers? I think those who are responsible for dealing with the spy question should take the same steps to protect the country against the possibility of trouble from spies as the military authorities are doing … I have a return here, not of Germans who are registered to- day, but of Germans who were registered in the Census returns three years ago, and it shows a very small proportion of people registered then as Germans compared with the number of Germans we now find to be in the country. I think I am right in saying that in England and Wales alone there were only about 13,800 as given in the Census returns, whereas now we know that there are something like 56,000. Of that number an enormous proportion were in Kent, Sussex, Essex particularly, and Yorkshire – all those counties along the East Coast of England. Hon. Members may laugh, but why did those men go and settle there, unless it was with some intention of being useful to their own friends if and when the day came, possibly even of an invasion of Great Britain. The Home Secretary has always been an optimist. He dealt with this matter last Session in the most optimistic spirit. He told us that nobody had been shot.

On the outbreak of war, the Home Secretary ordered that all German and Austrian subjects living in Britain had until 10 August to leave the country. Extraordinary as it seemed, the British government allowed German military reservists to travel freely to rejoin their regiments. On 5 August, the *Yorkshire Observer* reported that 'during the weekend quite a number of young Germans residing in Bradford left the city in order to rejoin their regiments. Yesterday about thirty departed for London on the 2.15pm train. They were seen off by friends and the German pastor.' Two weeks later, the same Bradford station saw more men with names like Muller, Hamlin, von Halle and Bernhardt leave, this time seen off by the Mayor, Chief Constable and a Colonel named Hoffman as they set out for officer training in the British army. Norman Muller, from Cononley, near Keighley, would die leading his troops into battle in 1918 and was the son of Colonel George Herbert Muller, the first commander of the Bradford Pals, and himself the son of a German immigrant. The following summer, Sir Richard Cooper told parliament that German names featured large in the ranks of the British army: 'In looking through the list of the staff in the War Office, in the July Army List, you will find such names as these, serving the country: Schlich, Bovenschen, Dannreuther, Rueker Munich, Underlin, Varrelmann, Ackermann, Umlauf. If anyone will take the trouble to look amongst the list of officers in the Army List for July, he will find that there are 135 officers whose names begin with 'Sch'. There is no really British name, to my knowledge which begins with 'Sch'. The Scholes and Schofield families who could trace their names back to the Middle Ages might disagree but the comments highlighted the difficulty in deciding who was truly 'British'. Even those who had formally taken British citizenship were suspect, with the *Daily Mail* asking 'Does signing his name take the malice out of a man?'

Those Germans not leaving to rejoin their regiments were given until 17 August to register at the local police station and Austrians had until the 23rd. Those who failed faced a possible £100 fine or six months' imprisonment, but part of the problem was that many 'aliens' did not realise they were foreigners. A statement of 'Advice to Aliens now in Britain' was produced by the government and published in local papers explained that 'British women who have married Germans have become German citizens and must be registered. The children of such marriages are in a similar position. Foreigners desirous to leave will find no difficulty unless German subjects if they provide themselves with passports etc and make sure beforehand of train and boat services ... Permits are only given to leave Britain by

German civilians of military age were rounded up by the authorities. Some would soon be released, others would spend the whole war in captivity.

Paul Cohen-Portheim was told to pack as if going on holiday and there was an air of unreality about the round-up.

certain ports on a given date by a given steamship service. Therefore those applying to leave should make sure of being able to leave a day or two before.' In other words, women and children who had never known anything other than life as British citizens became enemy aliens – 'hunwives' – overnight. Long queues of businessmen, nannies, students, tourists stranded by the war and old men and women who had left their homeland as children formed and stood patiently for hours before being processed.

Whipped up by rumour and wild stories, people began to see spies everywhere. The *Yorkshire Observer* of 15 August 1914 reported that 'a Rolls Royce of German registration was searched after its owners left for Germany and ... a large number of German and English maps were found in their car, together with detailed accounts of journeys made, a ruler, a whistle and a camera stand, some unused films and a quantity of rope. There were also a number of German newspapers with paragraphs marked in blue pencil relating to Irish Riots, insurrection in India, commercial war in England etc. ...' Ten days later *The Times* joined in, telling its readers in an editorial that 'many of the Germans still in London are unquestionably agents of the German government, however loose the tie may be … They had in their possession arms, wireless telegraph apparatus, aeroplane equipment, motor-cars, carrier pigeons and other material that might be useful to the belligerent … It has been remarked by the observant that German tradesmens' shops are frequently to be found in close proximity to vulnerable points in the chain of London's communications such as railway bridges…The German barber seems to have little time for sabotage. He is chiefly engaged in removing the 'Kaiser' moustaches of his compatriots. They cannot, however, part with the evidences of their nationality altogether, for the tell-tale hair of the Teuton will show the world that new Smith is but old Schmidt writ small.'

At a time when people were willing to believe that Russian soldiers were being transported from Scottish ports, during the warm August weather, to ports in Dover and arriving there with snow still on their boots, any story could find an audience. Soon people began to tear down adverts in the street for Maggi soup after rumours spread that German spies used them to pass messages, and the local pigeon racing club disbanded due to fears that its members might be suspected of using their birds to carry secrets. 'If you saw somebody in the street

Restrictions were put in place to prevent 'enemy aliens' travelling more than 5 miles from home. Charles Hagenbach was given a special permit.

that was a bit strange,' recalled Florence Mower, 'somebody perhaps with a black beard, kids would run after them shouting "You're a German spy." Someone you hadn't seen near your terrace before, who just happened to be looking around, was automatically a German spy.'

Victor Webb, a respectable Wakefield businessman, found himself in court in Southport in May 1915, charged under the Aliens Restriction Order and fined 40s after being found by police in a hotel room dressed in his wife's underwear and a wig. The landlady had been suspicious when 'Vera Cooper' had registered and complained about the 'nuisance' of having to fill in a registration form. With the papers full of tales of German spies dressed as women, poisoning water supplies and planning sabotage, Webb was taking a great risk for what he claimed was 'a joke', by then, the first of eleven German spies had been executed in the Tower of London, and several innocent civilians shot by enthusiastic sentries around the country. His defence solicitor told the court that his client was a British citizen and had simply been involved in 'a freak, a silly trick'. As if explaining everything, the *Liverpool Echo* of 17 May reported that he had 'been abroad several times and had done some amateur acting'.

In 1914, most towns had at least one or two German pork butcher shops and Wakefield was no exception, with shops run by Paul Andrassy, Frederick Gebhard, Martin Stwine and Charles Hoffman among others. They were often well established in the community but, like other small retailers, quickly became targets for anger at rising food prices. For the most part, though, Wakefield was spared the anti-German violence that broke out in some places. Although restrictions on travel were put in place, these shops were allowed to stay open as normal. Germans owning companies assisting in the war effort were also allowed to continue as 'supervised businesses' monitored by the authorities. The Swiss-born confectioner and baker Charles Hagenbach was able to obtain a pass proving he was not German, and, for him, life carried on as usual. From time to time problems cropped up – on 27 April 1915 Stanley musician Jacob Burro was sentenced to a fine of 40s or one month in prison for having travelled more than 5 miles from home without a permit, after going to Pontefract to help tent-maker George Andrassy to put up a marquee on the racecourse. Andrassy was given a £5 fine or two months for abetting. George Ziegler was fined in May 1915 for failing to blackout his shop properly but the court accepted it was unintentional and he was treated just as anyone else would have been. He was lucky. In May 1915, attitudes toward Germans – any Germans – were about to change.

During a crossing of the Atlantic from New York bound for Liverpool, the Cunard liner RMS *Lusitania* was spotted by a German submarine off the coast of Ireland, not far from the port of Cobh (from where the *Titanic* had left on its fateful voyage three years earlier). Germany had issued a warning in the United States that all shipping to Britain was at risk although few believed that a civilian ship would be targeted, especially one that carried many American passengers. The German threat was serious and the captain of U-20 ordered a single torpedo to be fired. Seconds after it hit, a second explosion was triggered in the ammunition stored in the *Lusitania*'s hold. The ship sank in just 20 minutes with the loss of 1,193 men, women and children, including 128 US citizens and three German stowaways reported to have been found soon after the ship set sail. The incident triggered a wave of anti-German violence across Britain, although the intensity varied. In the week after the attack Pontefract reported groups gathering near German-owned shops but no real violence whilst Castleford exploded into a full scale riot and at Goldthorpe a rioter was shot as he attacked a British-owned shop. Although the Mayor said that a country capable of such an atrocity should be 'wiped off the face of the earth', Wakefield remained relatively calm with only sporadic vandalism directed at small businesses. Typical of the sort of problems faced by these family businesses came in September, when cattle dealer Frederick Brook 'who was the worse for drink', and who had been 'in a heated discussion as to German "frightfulness"', smashed the windows at Hagenbach's shop and that of a nearby pork butcher, Charles Ziegler, with his walking stick, causing over £16 of damage. On arrest Brook said nothing to the police, instead breaking into a rendition of *Rule Britannia*. He was ordered to pay over £23 in compensation.

The *Lusitania* attack brought renewed concerns about what to do with the thousands of German, Austrian and other men of military age who had come to Britain from countries who were now deemed to be 'enemy aliens'. After the August 1914 registration date passed, men of military age were rounded up by police and army patrols until an assessment could be made of the level of threat they posed. Some of those previously released now found themselves re-arrested. Paul

Pork butchers' shops were a common target for anti-German anger.

Cohen-Portheim, a German-born Jew of Austrian parentage, was an artist and writer working in London at the start of the war. One of those rounded up after the sinking of the *Lusitania* in May 1915, he was told by the police to 'Pack as if you were going for a holiday' and filled two trunks in the hopes he would be gone a few days at most. In the morning, his last real friend in London accompanied him as far as the courtyard of the police station. From there he went by taxi to a camp in London's East End, where a thousand German and Austrian men of fighting age had been gathered together in an open hall. Given a metal disc with his prisoner number, Cohen-Portheim was relieved to learn he would only have to survive one night there. At six o'clock the next morning, armed guards marched the new prisoners through the streets of London to the train station as crowds lined their path, spitting, throwing things, and shouting about Huns and baby killers. At the train station, the nightmare suddenly ended as they boarded a comfortable train at the start of a journey that would take him first to the Isle of Man on the first stage of a 'holiday' that would last over three years.

Writing about his experiences, he described how easy it was to become a potential 'enemy':

The pride of our heart, however, remained with us Billie. Billie was 22, but looked 18 and the most typical English boy one could find anywhere. Which is exactly what he was. He was just a jolly English schoolboy with an irresistible smile who quite saw the fun of the situation. He could not speak a word of any language but English, and as to Germany he hardly knew it existed. He had never seen a German before he came to [the camp], but he made friends with everyone and was adored by most, certainly by all the 90 per cent who – as everywhere throughout the war were bad 'haters'. Billie's parents had emigrated to Australia when he was quite a little boy, and they had died out there. He had studied architecture and was passing his summer holiday in Europe. When war broke out he was in Belgium and came to England at once – without a passport, for before the war hardly anyone ever troubled to take out a passport, and even less to take one with him when travelling. Billie landed in Southampton and thought some of the buildings of that port quite interesting. So he started sketching them, and was promptly arrested, for the interesting buildings happened to be part of the fortifications. He had no papers, so the authorities decided he could only be a German. I imagine that even they must have thought him and his sketching too naive for a spy, but a German he would remain until he could prove another nationality, and so there he was amongst his 'compatriots'. He hoped to get his papers from Australia very soon, he told me, he had already waited ten months for them, meanwhile he intended to remain cheerful and did not despair of organizing football in the camp. Billie was not only popular on account of his charming smile, but also as a living proof of the utter lack of sense of the British authorities – which everyone felt they had shown in his own case as well – and because his presence consoled people in a way, for what could you expect if even Billie had been locked up! – I have often wondered if his papers ever arrived or what became of him.

Some prisoners were released once their case had been reviewed but sometimes it was too late, their livelihoods were gone. In February 1915, the House of Commons heard the story of Antonio Fell, a

BANDSTAND LOFTHOUSE PARK.

Lofthouse Park.

Conditions of Lofthouse Camp reflected the 10s each prisoner had to pay for the 'privilege' of being held there.

30-year-old Hungarian living in Nottingham, and married to an English wife. Fell had formerly worked as a a waiter in Nottingham for seven years and was interned at Wakefield in October 1914, but was released in December. Unable to resume his former employment and having exhausted his savings, Fell was now receiving 12s-6d a week from the local Board of Guardians. Would, asked MP Sir J.D. Rees, 'any action be taken to refund the expenditure incurred upon this alien, who has become a charge on the rates owing to action taken by Government arising out of the War?' Hundreds of innocent men had been rounded up, forced out of work and then, once it was realised they posed no threat, released to fend for themselves as best they could. But at least they could go home. Others would stay in prison without any sign of how long they would serve.

After a few months on the Isle of Man, Cohen-Portheim and around sixty other 'gentlemen prisoners' transferred to the special 'Zivilinternierungslager' (civilian internment camp) at Lofthouse Park, near Wakefield, a 'privilege' camp for the better off internees who could afford the 10s per week they would be charged for the dubious honour of being held prisoner there. Work on the camp had begun on 4 September 1914 when the government had announced its intention to take over Lofthouse Park for use as a prison camp. Built by the Yorkshire West Riding Electric Tramway Company and opening at Whitsuntide 1908, Lofthouse Park was one of Britain's first amusement parks and seemed an unlikely prison. The park had been built around a country house and its grounds, entered through a decorative arch lit by coloured light bulbs leading to a pavilion with a theatre and a cinema screen, a bandstand, a helterskelter, a privet hedge maze, a hall of mirrors and a haunted house called 'Kelly's Cottage', along with a roller skating rink. Around 200 Territorial soldiers of the 2nd West Riding Field Company of the Royal Engineers had been set to work to cut down the trees and bushes and to erect barbed wire fences and lighting to prepare the camp for the arrival of the first of an expected 1,000 prisoners in October.

The camp had three sub-divisions. First to be created was the south camp around the concert hall, which contained a stage and an auditorium and soon become a rabbit warren full of beds, chairs, clothes and men. As the camp filled, some wooden huts were added along with a hospital and barracks block. Later, a north camp was built using rows of long, low, wooden huts and there was a corrugated iron hall presented by an Anglo-German donor. Finally, a west camp of

Lofthouse Civilian Internment Camp.

corrugated iron huts was built on what was a treeless, grassless, waste ground adjoining the main camp. Each area was sealed and special permission was needed to move from one division to another. As a result, each developed its own character. Cohen-Portheim recalled how the South Camp housed men who had dealings in African colonies and who were 'inclined to be cranky'. The North Camp was 'rigid and correct' and regarded themselves as socially superior. He himself lived in the West Camp, which he felt 'had the least character and was the most colourless and monotonous of the three. It was essentially middle-class. Nearly all its inmates were businessmen who had lived in England before the war; a very few in a big way of business, but mostly men of moderate means. There was a majority of middle-aged, a minority of young men, mostly city clerks.' The exact status of the men held at Lofthouse was a matter of some debate. Although a few prisoners of war began to arrive in 1915, the majority of those held were not soldiers and so were not legally Prisoners of War. They had not committed a crime and so were not criminals. That made the question of how to deal with them a real problem.

Some were respectable and highly placed businessmen in engineering and other companies needed for the war effort.

Like British army officers held in German Prisoner of War camps, inmates could apply for 'parole', allowing them out of the camp for personal business. Captain Robert Campbell, for example, was even allowed to travel back to Britain for a fortnight from a German POW camp in November 1916 to visit his dying mother on condition he return to captivity afterwards. Having given his word, at the end of his allotted time, Captain Campbell duly made his way back to Magdeburg via neutral Holland and returned to captivity. In comparison, allowing German civilians out for day trips seemed reasonable enough to many. Those who gave their word returned to camp at the end of their paroles but there were others who were interested in a more permanent break from prison life.

On 1 June 1915, a report in the *Yorkshire Evening Post* of the mysterious disappearance of two prisoners from Lofthouse Camp, first noticed at roll call on 29 May. Lieutenant Colonel Gordon-Cumming, the Camp Commandant, refused to tell reporters what had happened other than to say that the wild speculation around how they had managed it was wrong. Some said that they had broken their parole whilst others thought they had walked out of the gate unnoticed by the guards. Locals said the fence was electrified so the notion that they had cut their way out was immediately dismissed. The mystery was solved later in the month when a report in a Stockholm newspaper and later the *Frankfurter Zeitung* described the adventures of Frederick Wiener and Alfred Klapproth after they walked out of the gates of Lofthouse and disappeared.

Wiener, aged 35, had settled in America and had been captured as he tried to make his way back to Austria. He had transferred to Lofthouse from a camp near Edinburgh and spoke English fluently with a strong American accent. Klapproth, aged 30, was a naval reservist who had been employed on Hamburg-Amerika Liners, and so spoke some English. Together the two men set about digging a tunnel out of the camp but gave up when they realised how long it would take. Instead, they hit upon a simple plan, they would walk out of the gate.

Having managed to get together about £30-worth of gold, they ordered new clothes from the camp tailor to make them look as British as possible. Wiener, at 5ft 11in and 'slight of figure' with a slight stoop, was last seen wearing a dark blue suit and a Tyrolese hat, whilst his stoutly-built friend wore a brown suit. They requested a meeting with the Camp Censor, knowing he would not be in at that time. From there, they went to the Guardroom where Wiener's English was good enough for him to claim they were both off-duty British officers and they then walked out, heading for Leeds and the railway station. There, they bought two first-class tickets to Manchester but travelled third class to Liverpool instead, spending their days wandering the streets and spending their nights in cafes and bars as they read about the intensive search for them in Manchester. After reading about Wiener's American accent, the two men switched to speaking French and passed themselves off as Frenchmen, even sending a postcard to the Commandant to tell him what they were doing. Eventually, they were able to persuade the crew of a Danish trawler, the *Tomsk*, to smuggle them to Copenhagen and from there made their way back to Germany.

Security immediately tightened up around Lofthouse but it was soon in the news again with the arrival in the camp of former Ambassador, Count Paul Wolf Metternich. Arrested on his honeymoon in August after marrying the daughter of an English admiral, the Count had been released but re-arrested by order of the Judicial Court and sent to special quarters in Lofthouse Camp. By now, the camp was the focus of attention, especially regarding the privileged lifestyle of men seen by the papers as enjoying 'many of the luxuries peculiar to a first class hotel'. Certainly, many locals saw the camp as more a resort than a prison and Frederick Booth, MP for Pontefract, asked the House of Commons whether it was 'aware that there are two kinds of treatment accorded in this camp, and that those who are inclined to be liberal in the way of tips are treated a great deal more leniently than the rest?'

A court case in April 1916 did little to help locals sympathise with the plight of the internees. Leeds-based wine and spirit merchants Hebblethwaite, Denham & Co. sued Richard Hartley, a market gardener at Lofthouse, for the return of empty bottles from the camp. Hartley, it was said, owed £11-10s and damages for failing to collect the '210 dozen' empties he should have returned to the suppliers, and a bemused court heard that some 'fifty to eighty dozen bottles of wine and spirits' were supplied to the prisoners every week. At a time when food shortages were beginning to bite this was a sore point for ordinary British civilians, particularly when compared to stories emerging from British prisoners of war in Germany of starvation in the camps.

As other reports filtered back about the conditions British soldiers were held under in German Prisoner of War camps, the seemingly luxurious conditions at Lofthouse came in for criticism, but however comfortable they might be, the men held there were still prisoners torn from their families and jobs with no foreseeable end to their sentence. In reality, the Geneva Convention demanded that prisoners be adequately fed on the same level of rations as soldiers. The British blockade was highly effective, leaving Germany so short of food that at Lofthouse's counterpart, Ruhleben Camp, near Berlin, by 1918 visiting wives and families frequently smuggled food *out* of the prison from supplies provided for their menfolk. By 1916, Lofthouse housed 1,322 Germans, 122 Austrians and three Turks and had grown to include a 3-acre sports field, fully-equipped gymnasium and eight tennis courts. Prisoners had arranged a full programme of lectures and classes that it was hoped would lead to recognised qualifications, there were painting and drawing clubs, gardens for each compound and a lively theatre group. Three kitchens provided meals with government rations supplemented by extras paid for by the men themselves. The camp was, according to an official report, for 'a superior class of men' and inspectors noted that 'the beef and Hamburger steaks ... attracted our particular attention on account of their excellence'.

'The horror of horrors,' wrote Paul Cohen-Portheim, 'the one which does not lessen with time but goes on increasing, is that you are never alone. Not by day, by night, not for a second, day after day, year after year – barbed wire disease – the monstrous, enforced incessant community with no privacy, no possibility of being alone, no possibility of finding quietude. It is not the men of bad character or morals you begin to hate but the men who draw their soup through their teeth, clean their ears with their fingers at dinner, hiccough unavoidably when they get up from their meal (a moment awaited with trembling fury by the other), the man who will invariably make the same remark (day after day, year after year) as he sits down, the man who lisps, the man who brags ... silly trifles get on your nerves and become unendurable by the simple process of endless repetition. So grows an atmosphere of mutual dislike, suspiciousness, meanness, hatred. Men become deadly enemies over a piece of bread.'

First recorded by A.L. Vischer, an inspector from the Swiss Embassy in London, 'Barbed wire disease', a form of psychological breakdown began to appear. The first signs would usually be some peculiar behaviour or outbursts of temper. The man would lose his interests, become solitary and perhaps start muttering to himself or waving his fingers. Common symptoms were suspicion of comrades, delusions of persecution or disease, loss of memory and poor concentration. In serious cases the man could be subject to outbreaks of hysteria and raving. Few men interned for six months or more did not show at least some signs of psychological harm as a result and some found it all too much. In April 1915, 39-year-old former Manchester hotel waiter Herman Kraus cut his own throat with his razor and died 8 minutes after being found in the lavatories at Lofthouse.

The presence of so many aristocratic and well connected internees made Lofthouse a very difficult place to manage. The 'Gentlemen' could not be treated like common prisoners and many had connections within the British government that made discipline hard to enforce. After the escape, paroles were expected to be escorted, but echoing Frederick Booth's comments about tipping, in 1918 the Camp's British Quartermaster, Lieutenant Albert Canning was court-martialed, charged with breaches of military discipline following an argument with the Camp Commandant, Lieutenant Colonel Haines. Over dinner one evening, Canning told Haines that, in his opinion, 'you have only to be a Baron in this camp to be treated in a preferential manner', and accused the Colonel of failing in his duties. The trigger had the visits of Mrs Leverton Harris, wife of the Parliamentary Secretary to the Ministry of Blockade, to Baron Leopold von Plessen, and by other ladies to Count Metternich and Count Nettenblad. Mrs Harris had been given permission by the Home Office to visit the Baron at the request of an American aunt of his but had insisted on her visits not being supervised or time limited as others were. Lieutenant Canning claimed to have overheard her telling the Baron that 'when this wretched war is over, how happy we shall be', and said that he thought she might be in love with him despite being 'old enough to be his mother, if not his grandmother'. In the course of the trial it emerged that the Baron had been involved in an escape attempt but had not lost privileges as a result and that he had been allowed unsupervised visits on the strength of letters from Mrs Harris' husband. Lieutenant Canning was acquitted.

In what must have been an entertaining debate in 1918, Earl Grey informed the House of Lords of a conversation reported to him by an anonymous source in Bradford who claimed to have overheard an exchange between a local businessman and an interned German out on parole: 'The conversation which was overheard was that between an interned German and a very prominent partner in what is called a supervised firm, which has been officially declared to be beyond suspicion on more than one occasion recently. I will attempt to read the conversation as it is written in the sort of English which our naturalised aliens use. The interned German said – "Well, ou arrr yu koin onn een Praatfort?" And this was the reply – "Hoch, fein! Ve arrr orl rreit. I sink orl Inglisschmen moost pee tampt phools; der Vor can ko hon for ass longg ass eet leike – ve arrr orl ferry 'appy an mekking mooch munny; vu haf no hinterranses voteffer."' The main issue for Grey was why a firm partly owned by a German was facing no 'hinterranses' in completing business orders placed by the British government. There were many such 'supervised' businesses still in operation and working on military contracts overseen by the Ministry of Production but there were also many others competing for contracts. The report, complete with its exaggerated accent, was traced to a rival company.

As the war drew on, more military prisoners arrived and after the Armistice it became a holding centre for German officers. Civilian internees were released, some to go home, others facing repatriation. Frederich Brandauer, a 56-year-old millionaire who owned a pen company, and who had lived in England for thirty years, took poison at a camp on the Isle of Man rather than be forcibly repatriated to Germany. The winter of 1918–19 saw a rash of similar stories from camps around the country as men faced the threat of being forced out of their adopted home to a country many of them could barely remember. For others, a return home was the most important thing in their lives. Even with nowhere to go after the war ended, German officers made several attempts to tunnel out of Lofthouse, with the last being discovered when an alert sentry heard the sounds of digging below his feet in November 1919. It was hardly worth the effort – the camp was reported to be empty by the end of December as the last prisoners left on their way to Hull and home.

For thousands of civilians, both in Britain and Germany, the war was spent in a limbo brought about by the problem of working out whether what mattered was where someone was born or where they chose to belong – a problem that a century later is emerging yet again. After the war, Paul Cohen-Portheim returned to writing and described his experiences in his book *Time Stood Still*. The title was carefully chosen: for him, the war was almost four years in which 'the past was dead, the future, if there should be a future, was a blank, there was nothing left but the present, and my present was the life of a prisoner ... where there is no aim, no object, no sense, there *is* no time.' Yet whilst their fathers languished in prison for the crime of being foreign, their sons were being forced to do their duty for Britain as the Military Service Act came into force, and told them that if their parents were enemy aliens and hunwives, they themselves were British enough to be conscripted.

CHAPTER 4

Conscripts and Conchies

The British Expeditionary Force (BEF) sent to France in August 1914 was soon forced to retreat as the huge German army threatened to overwhelm it, and by the end of August it had been pushed back almost to the gates of Paris, with a German victory seeming to be entirely possible, even likely. A special edition of *The Times*, on Sunday, 30 August, carried a report from France that spoke of 'Broken British Regiments' and reflected the fact that over 15,000 trained men of the professional pre-war army had already been lost in the retreat from Mons and the remainder were still suffering heavy losses daily. By the end of the year, about one in three of the entire British army's strength were casualties. Realising that the army would need to expand massively if it was to play any realistic part in fighting the enormous numbers of men the German and Austro-Hungarian empires could send to the front, the newly appointed Secretary of State for War, Lord Kitchener, began planning the creation of what would become known as the 'New Army'.

Conditioned by some twenty years of newspaper propaganda to believe that Germany was poised to invade Britain, and that many east European immigrants were really German agents waiting to rise up in support of that invasion, thousands of young men rushed to enlist, believing that their homes and families were in immediate danger. For some it was their patriotic duty to defend their homeland, but for many it was an opportunity and excuse to escape from dull jobs and join in the great adventure overseas. In the first week of September, over 900 Wakefield men were accepted into the forces, 600 following the recruiting rallies held outside the Town Hall. Fifty-two council employees led the way. Across the country just under 463,000 men enlisted in September alone, joining the 299,000 who had enlisted in August and together completely swamping the system set up for the pre-war army that was designed to accept, equip and train fewer than 30,000 men per year and able to house only around

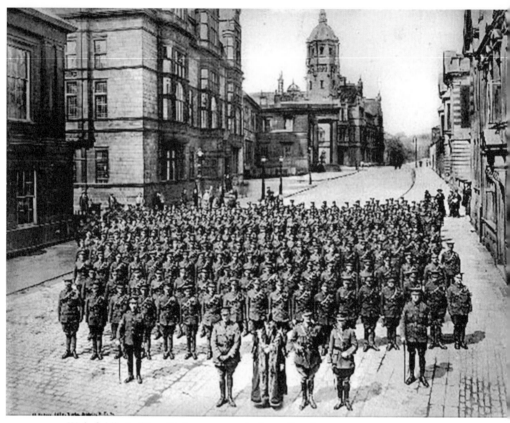

Wakefield's Artillery Battery prepare to leave the city.

177,000 soldiers in total. With so many enlisting, checks were basic and the enlistment forms only asked for the recruits 'apparent age' so that any young man choosing to add a few months or even a year or two to his age could probably slip through. The minimum age for joining the Territorial Force was 17, the Regulars 18 and for service overseas it was 19 and the 'apparent' difference between them was not always obvious. Today, the issue of 'underage' soldiers in the First World War remains emotive but almost forgotten are the others who also lied – Lieutenant Henry Webber served on the Somme, out-ranked by two sons with the rank of Major and a third son a Colonel. He died from a head wound in 1916 at the age of 67, having taken twenty-five years off his age to enlist in 1914. It was technically illegal, but the army did not prosecute those it caught, arguing that many from poorer families might not have birth certificates and so couldn't actually know how old they really were.

As a result of the flood of volunteers, reports began to filter back of scenes of chaos at the Pontefract Barracks, home to both the King's Own Yorkshire Light Infantry and the York and Lancaster

"WHERE DUTY AND GLORY LEAD."

161st BRIGADE
(YORKSHIRE)

ROYAL FIELD ARTILLERY.

The City of Wakefield has received authority
to raise from the District

A BATTERY

AND AN

AMMUNITION COLUMN.

As only a limited number of Men are
required for this Splendid Arm of the Service
application for enlistment should be made
without delay.

	Age	Chest meas. ins.	Height ft. ins.
Gunners :	19 to 38	35	5-7 to 5-10
Drivers :	19 to 38	35	5-3 to 5-7

Pay and Allowances at Army Rates.
Service—Duration of the War.

RECRUITING OFFICE : 7, BANK ST., WAKEFIELD.

Hours : 8 a.m. to 8 p.m.

Sondeson & Clayton, Printers, Wakefield.

As the army expanded, new units were formed and adverts similar to this became a
regular feature in local newspapers.

regiments. Not surprisingly, supplies of beds, uniforms, equipment and even food soon began to run out at regimental depots everywhere. Some men were billeted with local families or even stayed at home, commuting to the army just as they had to work. Others camped out in any available buildings whilst more slept in tents pitched around the barracks as the harassed depot staff struggled to maintain any sort of order. Many men simply walked away and went home for their meals or to visit families for the weekend, often without their absence being noticed. Those who lived too far away stayed put and complaints began to appear in local papers about conditions at the depot. On 26 September, under the heading 'Life at Pontefract Camp – Silly Rumours Contradicted', the *Dewsbury Reporter* received a letter from a group of local men:

> Many rumours have been circulated in the district regarding the conditions under which our local soldiers are housed at Pontefract and the treatment they have received with regard to food etc. The following letter has come to hand this week, and we trust that it will put an end to the ridiculous tales: 'To the Editor of the Reporter, Sir, – Having heard that there have been many rumours about that the Pontefract camp is in a filthy condition and that there is not enough to eat for the soldiers, we, the undersigned, wish to contradict these rumours. We are all Batley chaps who have been at Pontefract for three weeks, and we are all in the pink of condition and ready for anything. The camp is cleared up and disinfected every day, and as for eating, we have enough and to spare. For breakfast we have bread and butter – not margarine – and jam and cheese; to dinner we have boiled beef, fresh every day, along with cabbage and carrots; and for tea we get bread and butter, tinned salmon and tinned herrings or potted beef: so you will see whether we are pined or not'.

If the food was good, the sheer scale of the effort of creating a New Army from scratch meant that recruits spent a lot of time sitting around waiting for things to happen. Restrictions on pub opening times around military buildings were strictly enforced and so, with nothing much to do and nowhere to entertain themselves when off-duty, bored soldiers began to desert in order to enlist in other regiments where the prospects of action seemed better. Others simply tagged on to drafts of men being sent off to training camps around the country and hoped no-one would notice the extra bodies. Wakefield men began to turn up in regiments that seemed odd choices for Yorkshiremen. Posted from Tralee in Ireland to Pontefract Barracks, Captain Godfrey Drage of the Royal Munster Fusiliers decided to use the chaos there to his own regiment's advantage:

> I realised that I had very little idea how many men the Munsters could possibly absorb. However, a thousand seemed a good round number and so I announced, 'I'm only authorised to take a thousand of you'. Then I made them strip to the waist and walked down the ranks feeling each man's biceps and asking what he was in civil life. If he said 'I'm a miner' I took him without more ado. So far I'd got away with everything but, by the time I'd got 500 lined up the Adjutant of the depot heard about my goings on and came running up – 'Here I say Captain Drage, you can't do that! You're taking all my best men'. I thought I'd better not ride my luck too far and so I saluted very subserviently and replied, 'Yes sir, certainly sir, would you like to choose the rest yourself sir?' He did so and you can imagine what the next 500 were like. Anyway, I'd got my draft and thought I'd better be off while the going was good.

More were persuaded to join the Connaught Rangers, whilst 500 more who had signed up for the KOYLI or the York and Lancasters had served only a week before they allowed themselves to be talked out of the army altogether and poached to serve as infantry in the newly formed Royal Naval Division, marching proudly out of Pontefract led by the Church Boys' Brigade band. Gradually, though, the system began to work itself out. As more and more battalions of the KOYLI and York and Lancasters were formed, drafts of around 300 men each were put together and sent on their way to camps scattered around the country.

With the existing battalions full, the War Office began to create new 'Service' battalions that would be added to the strength of regiments for the duration of the war. From just five battalions in 1914, the KOYLI would eventually be responsible for twenty-two, a growth dwarfed by the City of London Regiment, which grew from seven to forty-nine battalions in less than two years. In many towns, especially across the industrial north, local authorities sponsored their own units, paying for food, accommodation and training until the War Office could accept them as soldiers. These 'Pals' battalions encouraged men to enlist so they could serve alongside others from their

Pontefract Barracks.

home town and neighbouring cities competed to produce the best soldiers.

Among the groups attempting to raise their own battalion were the West Yorkshire Coal Owners Association (WYCOA), who put aside £22,000 for the purpose and began recruiting at pits across Yorkshire, but struggled to find enough men willing to join what was already being referred to as the 'Pontefract Battalion'. Many miners had already enlisted but many more fell foul of the new regulations raising the minimum height requirement from 5ft 2ins to 5ft 6ins. Given the difficulties, the WYCOA considered simply donating £10,000 to the War Office instead, but when they approached them, the War Office agreed to waive the rules and to draft in extra numbers from among the other KOYLI volunteers, provided they would be treated the same as their miner comrades. It also offered to provide £7-5s per man for equipment and 2s a day for food. Thus encouraged, the WYCOA went back to recruiting what was now being referred to as the 12th (Service) Battalion (Yorkshire Miner's) of the King's Own Yorkshire Light Infantry or, more simply, 12 KOYLI. By the end of the year, a full battalion was in training at Farnley Park near Leeds.

But if thousands came forward to volunteer and were accepted into the army, many thousands more did not. There were many reasons: some with families simply could not afford the pay cut to the shilling a day that a soldier received; some were running small businesses and would lose everything if they enlisted; some had elderly or sick family members who needed to be looked after. Increased height and medical standards had been put in place to try to slow the flood of recruits and eager volunteers discovered that even a stammer or bad teeth could be cause for rejection. It was estimated that a typical working-class 15-year-old was up to 4 inches (10cm) shorter than his middle-class counterpart, and malnutrition in poorer areas meant that a high percentage of those coming forward had some form of physical problem that would affect their ability to serve. As a result, enlistment for some meant perseverance, sometimes travelling from town to town in search of a recruiter willing to take them on. In March 1915, the *Sheffield Independent* newspaper reported on a letter from a soldier at the Voluntary Aid Detachment hospital in Wakefield describing a fellow patient. In amongst the men recovering from wounds received in France was a local civilian, 43-year-old father of six Henry 'Harry' Kirby of Berners Street. Harry had lied about his age (he was over maximum age for volunteers) when he attempted to enlist, only to be rejected at the medical. The doctor advised him that an operation would make him fit for service and so he duly went off to undergo two operations and recover at the VAD hospital so that he could, as he told his fellow patients 'have a pop at the Germans' and, according to the letter writer, the wounded men around him 'are all proud of him as we think he is made of the right stuff'. Harry got his wish, arriving in France in November 1915 with the Royal Field Artillery. Both Harry and his eldest son Alan, a sailor in the Royal Navy, survived the war.

European armies had relied for generations on conscription to fill their ranks. A young man would be required to complete military training and serve for a period as a soldier. Once he had completed his service, he would remain a Reservist, liable for recall in times of national emergency, and later for recall to a reserve or home defence unit. That meant that those countries not only had a standing army ready immediately in times of war, but that they also had a huge pool of trained men available for call up at short notice who would not need to be trained and could be sent immediately to the front. For over a century, British generals and politicians had argued the need

WAKEFIELDER'S PLUCK.

EAGERNESS TO HAVE A POP AT THE GERMANS.

An incident illustrating the pluck of a Wakefield young man who was anxious to join the colours has been drawn attention to by a wounded soldier in the V.A.D. Hospital, at Wakefield, who in a letter signs himself "One Who Admires Him." In the course of the letter he states:—

"In the ward at this hospital occupied by wounded soldiers from the front we have a Wakefield man who is evidently made of the right sort of stuff. He was anxious to enlist, but was told that he could not be accepted unless he underwent an operation. He gladly consented to this, and he has undergone two operations, as he is eager to get well in order (as he says) to have a pop at the Germans. We are all proud of him, as we think he is made of the right stuff.

"His name is Harry Kirby—a married man with a wife and six children—and he lives at Berners street, Wakefield. What do the young ones think of this?"

Sheffield Independent, 13 March 1915.

for a similar system but without success and now it was too late. The heady rush of recruits in August and September 1914 could not be maintained and the goal set by Kitchener of an army of seventy divisions would not be met by relying on volunteers alone. That would have required 92,000 new recruits per month at a time when recruiting figures were dropping. The obvious answer was conscription but the government was unwilling to introduce such an unpopular step.

The problems of recruitment for the Boer War had brought the conscription debate back to the surface and the years leading up to the outbreak of war saw an outpouring of books, reports and other propaganda foretelling of the consequences of failing to keep the army strong. No government, though, was willing to even consider imposing conscription in peacetime and even in a state of emergency, the risks were high. Around 40 per cent of males over the age of 21 were not eligible to vote and would not tolerate being ordered to fight for a government they had no say in choosing.

To counter the arguments of trade unions and others, workers had to be convinced that if there were too few volunteers to meet the need, Britain would lose the war and the country would be forced to accept German rule. It was becoming increasingly obvious that the voluntary system was breaking down and, as one observer noted, by mid 1915 'the average recruiting speech became a mixture of abuse, cajolery and threats ... the men secured by pressure of this kind could hardly be described as volunteers ... the whole business has become manifestly unfair ... men were induced to join whose business and family obligations ought to have secured them a respite, while insensitive people with no such responsibilities smiled and sat tight'. On the one hand, the government needed to ensure that essential industries carried on and that men with specialist skills remained at home. Calling up every man would dilute the workforce and the impact on business would risk leaving Britain bankrupt. On the other, men at the front complained bitterly about having to shoulder a heavy burden whilst 'shirkers' stayed safely at home. By then it was increasingly clear that something needed to be done.

With both military and industrial needs in mind, a new proposal was put forward to ensure that the government was able to make best use of the skills and talents of its population by ordering that every individual's suitability for undertaking war work must be registered. Despite widespread acceptance that this was just a step away from conscription, the National Registration Act passed its third reading with only token opposition in July. Sunday, 15 August 1915, was designated as Registration Day when all citizens, male or female, between the ages of 15 and 65 were required, under penalty of law, to report to canvassers their names, occupations, details of current employment, family circumstances and any skills useful to war work. The information gathered from male respondents between the ages of 18 and 41 was copied onto pink forms (white forms were used for

MILITARY SERVICE ACT, 1916

Every man to whom the Act applies will on Thursday, March 2nd be deemed to have enlisted for the period of the War unless he is excepted or exempt.

Any man who has adequate grounds for applying to a Local Tribunal for a

CERTIFICATE OF EXEMPTION UNDER THIS ACT

Must do so BEFORE

THURSDAY, MARCH 2

Why wait for the Act to apply to you?

Come _now_ and join of your own free will. You can at once put your claim before a Local Tribunal for exemption from being called up for Military Service if you wish.

ATTEST NOW

WITH FOND GREETINGS

FROM A MUNITION WORKER

HELPING TO "CARRY ON"

THIS BADGE proves
I'm A "WORKER"
Who can ne'er be
dubbed a "shirker,"
And my output proves
that I have put on speed,
So with pride my Badge
I'll wear
To prove I do my share—
For Country, and the Lads,
when they're in need.

With conscription about to be introduced, specialist war workers had to prove that they were of more use in a factory than in France.

females and blue denoted males not of military age or fitness), with the cards of men employed in necessary occupations marked with black stars and subsequently referred to as 'starred' occupations.

For the benefit of trade union leaders, a list of 'starred' occupations was published in the papers. Unless it could be shown that they could not be replaced by women or men ineligible for military service, builders involved in the construction of munitions works or other military buildings, textile workers working on military contracts, munitions workers, railwaymen and other transport staff and a variety of other trades including bootmakers, saddlers, tent-makers, horse breeders and motor vehicle makers were all exempt. By the end of October, the information gathered had been analysed and revealed that there were 5,158,211 men recorded on pink forms, with only 1,519,432 of them starred. Further reducing the number available by the accepted average of 25 per cent for medical rejection, this left a manpower pool of about 2.7 million available for the military.

Now armed with concrete evidence, Lloyd George and the Munitions Ministry could show that the country could not afford to lose any more skilled men to voluntary enlistment, but that there was a significant pool of available manpower that could be used to reinforce the army. The main problem was one of how to introduce the scheme against opposition from powerful trade unions who had already shown themselves willing to take strike action that harmed the war effort and widespread hostility from the general public. The response, made public on 19 October, was the compromise 'Derby Scheme'. Under the control of Lord Derby, the newly appointed head of the Joint Recruiting Committee of the War Office, all those listed by the National Registration Act as being between the ages of 19 to 41 in England, Wales and Scotland were banded into one of forty-six age classifications, twenty-three each for married and unmarried men. Each was to be offered the chance either to enlist directly or to attest their willingness to serve in the army when called at a later date, in a kind of 'fall or be pushed' final opportunity to join up as a volunteer. The scheme stressed that workers in relevant trades deemed to be of national importance would be attested but would not actually be called up as long as they carried on working in those trades and that unmarried men would be called up first. All men who attested, regardless of skills, received 2s-6d and a special armband signifying their new status to provide protection against the growing hostility towards shirkers. Skilled men in key trades also received special armbands declaring their work to be a special contribution to the war effort. Tribunals would be set up to hear individual appeals for exemption or deferment.

In Wakefield, rooms in schools were set aside for use by the organisers of the Derby Scheme and the West Riding Education Committee agreed that teachers and attendance officers could be used to assist in administration, although the committee was not able to agree to release teachers if called up. By November, the *Yorkshire Post* was able to claim that Wakefield was doing well and that 'in a very short time there will not be a single young fellow in the city who can say if "unstarred" that he has not been personally asked to give his services in this crisis'. Figures for Wakefield itself, were not available, but Dewsbury had reported fewer than sixty responses in the previous week and returns across the larger towns and cities were steady but far below the numbers needed. Potential recruits in Leeds were required to produce their identity papers after the authorities became aware that men were coming forward several times to collect the day's pay offered to every recruit coming forward.

Although presented as a success, few people saw the scheme as anything but a stepping stone to wide-scale compulsory military service and the results were disappointing. Married men, assured they would not be called until after the single men, attested in greater numbers but even then only around half came forward. It was the proof the government needed that it could no longer rely on voluntary enlistment and even as Lord Derby worked hard to oversee the last stage of voluntary enlistment, a Military Service Act introducing conscription was already working its way through Parliament. The first draft of the new act went before the Cabinet on 1 January 1916, just two weeks after the closing date for registration under the Derby Scheme, and on 27 January 1916 compulsory military service was introduced for every male who 'on 15 August 1915 was ordinarily resident in Great Britain and who had attained the age of 19 but was not yet 41 and – on 2 November 1915 was unmarried or a widower without dependent children'.

Under the terms of the 'Bachelor's Bill', as it became known, unless they met certain exceptions or had reached the age of 41 before the appointed date, from 2 March 1916 all unmarried men in the country were deemed to have enlisted for general service with the colours or in the reserve and were, for the time being, regarded as being in the reserve. Each man was allocated into a class relating to the year of his birth, ranging from Class 1 (1896) to Class 23 (1875), and would be called forward according to that class, with the youngest not expected to be called until they reached their 19th birthday. A public proclamation would be posted announcing the call up of each class and each man would receive an individual call-up notice. Those with a preference for service in the navy could state it and would be offered to the Admiralty. Tribunals would be put in place to hear appeals or requests for exemptions and deferments where service would cause severe hardship to a family or business or where a man had a conscientious objection to the military. By March 1916, Sir William Robertson, Britain's senior soldier, complained that of 'the 193,891 men called up under the Military Service Act, no fewer than 57,146 have failed to appear'.

In order to allow for those special cases where a man had strong religious

A War Service badge issued to essential workers.

grounds for not wanting to serve or where a family would suffer severe hardship by having someone taken by the army, around 1,800 tribunals were set up around the country where local union representatives, shopkeepers, magistrates and other members of the community sat in long sessions listening to appeals for exemption, sometimes for the flimsiest of reasons. Wakefield Council's General Purposes Committee met on 9 February 1916 and appointed the ageing Alderman William H. Kingswell, who was the proprietor of a large store in the centre of town specialising in ladies' clothing, furs and curtaining, and whose solicitor son would often represent applicants. Alongside Kingswell would be Alderman George A. Moorhouse, Councillor Benjamin Hale, Henry Chalker (the clerk to the Wakefield magistrates who would act as Chairman) and Thomas B. Sugden, the Registrar at the West Riding Registry of Deeds. These five would form the core of the tribunal for the rest of the war. Representing the military would be the local recruiting officer, Major L.J.P. Watson and later J.B. Cooke (described as the National Service representative), who would put the case for calling up. After the war all records were destroyed and local newspaper reports rarely named individuals, but a picture of the sort of applicants coming to the tribunals can be gained from regular accounts in the *Wakefield Express* and other newspapers.

The Wakefield Tribunal began work and its first three applicants were all young men who claimed to be supporting their widowed mothers. One worked at a maltkiln and gave his mother 27s a week of the 31s he earned. Another was a colliery clerk giving his mother 28s. The third, a colliery banksman, told the tribunal that he provided his mother with £1 a week. All claimed that if they were called up or even worse killed, their mothers would be dependent on charity. They were told that the army would provide an allowance for dependants and they must accept the call-up. The number of appeals from the sons of local businessmen needing exemptions to allow them to take over the family firms from frail fathers, led one Lancashire observer to note drily that 'senile decay sets in at a very early age in Preston' and separating genuine cases of potential hardship from those simply finding excuses to avoid service was a thankless task. The work was made even more difficult by the letters they received from disgruntled wives asking for their menfolk to be taken away on the grounds that they were sick of them being at home and felt a spell in the army would be good for them, or from angry neighbours demanding that a nearby 'shirker' be taken.

The tribunal was in place to weigh up the pros and cons of each individual case against the need for men at the front. They were very much aware that for each man appearing before them saying that he was needed by his family at home, there were mothers and fathers with sons already serving and the question was one of deciding why all men shouldn't be expected to be treated equally by the army. There was also a need to examine whether the cases were concerned more with self interest than the national good. The first employers to come before the Tribunal, for example, were brothers who ran an 11-acre business as florists, seedsmen and market gardeners. Three of their men had already joined up and they were seeking exemption for one of the other two. Arguing that he could not be replaced, under questioning they admitted that they had not even tried advertising for anyone to replace him. They were given three months to find someone over military age. Other cases were brought on behalf of individuals by their employers but in March Chairman Mr T. Norton angrily told them to stop claiming they had 'given' or 'sent' men to the army because the fact was that the army had taken them. It was ridiculous, he said, for employers to suggest they had been generous enough already as part of their case for retaining a particular employee. In many cases, the tribunal argued, these were jobs that did not need a fit, healthy military age man but could be done equally well by older men or by women.

So when, in May, South Kirby and Hemsworth Collieries Ltd appealed on behalf of a 28-year-old costs clerk on the grounds that they had lost 40 per cent of their clerks, the Tribunal were less than sympathetic to the argument. It emerged that 'no effort had been made to secure female clerks as they were considered unsuitable. The Chairman said female clerks worked in banks and he did not see why they could not work in colliery offices and the appeal was refused. Another young clerk was living with three unmarried sisters, only one of whom went out to work. He said that he contributed 25s a week to the family budget but Alderman Kingswell told him that his other sisters could find employment and earn £1 a week at E. Green & Son in Calder Vale Road, who had branched out from making fuel economisers into munitions work and were employing a great many women. A Wakefield chimney sweep asked for exemption for his son who, he emphasised, cleaned the chimneys of the workhouse, the prison and the pauper lunatic asylum at Stanley Royd Hospital. Women, he said, were good for cleaning floors, but not for sweeping chimneys. The Tribunal chairman, Henry Chalker, told him in no uncertain terms that they 'were only just beginning to find out what women were really capable of'. The sweep was given three months to find someone to replace the boy.

Dairymen and farmers in particular were desperately short of labour and often came before the Tribunal to plead for exemption for their remaining men. By 1917, a 'Women's Land Service Corps' had been formed but in the early days there were two problems: firstly, was the need to persuade farmers to employ women and secondly to persuade women to work on farms. Lady Catherine Milnes Gaskell, of Thornes House, a member of the Wakefield Rural District's War Agricultural Sub-Committee amongst her other posts, told a gathering of farmers that they must realise that the war was on a 'more colossal scale' than anything previously known. They must, she continued, both grow more food and free their men for active service. A representative of the National Farmers Union accepted that women might be able to do some jobs but, he insisted, they would never be able to put manure onto carts. Lady Catherine and her friend Lady Kathleen Pilkington, of Chevet Hall, canvassed local women to gather recruits to train as farmworkers but had not reckoned on the fact that town women were simply not interested in walking miles to work on the land in all weathers when they could earn better money doing munitions work closer to home.

Often hearing eighty or more cases per sitting, the Wakefield Tribunal worked hard to try to balance individual and local needs with national ones. Exemptions were made wherever a reasonable case of genuine need could be proven, such as the application by the West Riding's Acting Chief Constable, Mr A.C. Quest, for the exemption of seventy-three unattested police officers, all of whom were considered essential. It was granted provided as long as they continued to be serving policemen. The Wakefield Gaslight Company was also able to achieve exemption for large numbers of its employees on the grounds that they had all required extensive training for skilled work and had already given many years of service. Such vital experience could not be readily replaced and as most local people depended on gas for their home power supply, it was considered essential to keep the men at home.

The Yorkshire (West Riding) Electric Tramway Company had taken over the Wakefield and District Light Railway Company in 1905 and ran all trams around the district and General Manager H. England, himself of military age, appeared before the tribunal many times to argue cases for his staff in an increasingly desperate attempt to maintain a reasonable service. A long-running debate developed around how far the service could be cut back and to what extent it could be expected to rely on women or men too old for military service to replace its trained drivers, inspectors and engineers. In July 1916, England sought exemption for some eighty employees including clerical staff, drivers, engineers, four inspectors and the chief inspector. The appeal was allowed in the majority of cases but the tribunal insisted that a driver who was a single man and only 20 years old must join the armed services along with two track workers. Three months later Edwards appeared again, seeking exemption for twenty-seven men, most of whom were drivers. He argued that men were being called up who were not really fit, a view shared by tribunal chairman Kingswell who said, 'I think myself that there are men who are called up for military service now who would break down in a short time and who will cost the country a great deal in hospital or be sent back to ordinary employment.' However, he also had to accept that the Tribunal could not 'go behind the certificate of the proper medical authorities'. Exemption was refused for four of the men who were both young and single. The cases of the married men were to be further investigated with the military representative.

By the time England came before the Tribunal again in October 1916, conductors had already been replaced by women and he tried to plead the case for two men, aged 24 and 27, who ran the trams, carrying hundreds of men from Rothwell to work each day. It was not in the interests of the country to take them from their job, he argued, because he had already stopped the late trams and could make no further cuts. He was so short of drivers that if one were absent, an inspector had to take the tram. He explained that he had tried using women as drivers but one had fainted and the other had simply run away, leaving her tram driverless. Other companies, he claimed, had been allowed to keep all their drivers and repairmen.

Some idea of the Tramway Company employees' experiences at this time come from a surviving file of the manager's correspondence. Albert Sharp lived in Rhodes Terrace, Kirkgate and was employed to work on mechanical and electrical repairs to the trams. Sharp had attested under Lord Derby's scheme and received a letter in January 1916 requiring him to present himself for active service on 9 February. England wrote to Major Watson immediately to say that Sharp was necessary to the company for the proper conduct of its business, that it would be impossible to replace him and that losing him would cause considerable inconvenience. Watson agreed that he was in a reserved occupation but in July, Sharp was called up again and England made another appeal on his behalf. Letters show that Sharp was very conscious that young men in the street not wearing military uniform were a target of growing anger and that England advised him to carry his medical certificate and registration card with him at all times, 'as you may be expected to produce these for the inspection of a police officer. Should you be accosted by the military authorities, you can inform them that we have entered an appeal for you before the Wakefield Tribunal but that the Tribunal have not yet dealt with the appeal'. Sharp was again granted exemption but was called up for a third time in December. This time he was granted exemption only until a substitute could be found. Major Watson found someone suitable in March 1917 and at last Sharp joined the army, serving in the Royal West Kent Regiment. It is a measure of how seriously England took his role that after the war he tried to re-employ Sharp. He wrote to him in January 1919, offering him work and, having heard nothing by March, he went so far as write to the manager of Wakefield Labour Exchange to ask him if he could speed up Sharp's discharge, and he returned to the Company as a relief handyman in April. Despite the efforts on his behalf, though, papers in the file suggest that he was not a particularly good worker.

Finding a way to balance business needs was a continuing theme of the tribunal's work. In June, problems arose around which Wakefield butchers should be regarded as essential and who could be released for military service. The Leeds Butchers Association had set up its own tribunal using members of the association elected by all members eligible for call up to make the difficult decision. In Wakefield, though, butchers could not 'decide amicably among themselves' who should form the tribunal and each member had to apply to the official appeal system on an individual basis. Rising meat prices, noted the *Yorkshire Evening Post* of 6 June 1916, meant that it was likely that some would go out of business anyway. 'The tendency, at any rate, is toward fewer shops and this lightens the task of the butchers private tribunal'. One firm of meat dealers went so far as to lodge appeals at both Leeds and Wakefield in an attempt to retain managers of its shops in Wombwell and Normanton, a practice regarded as unfair and led to demands that appeals should be restricted to tribunals who understood local conditions.

A month later, the manager of the Wakefield Industrial Society asked for exemption for fourteen men, most of whom were branch managers. The Society had grown considerably since it foundation and had branches in many areas on the outskirts of the city and as far away as Crofton, Featherstone and Kinsley and had already lost 44 of its 143 male employees, all of whom had been examined that morning at Pontefract and found fit for service. Alderman Kingswell was scathing about the application, telling them that independent retailers had already suffered the loss of many of their male employees and could be put out of business if the Cooperative Society were allowed to keep all the men it wanted. Major Watson advised that the Society must 'consolidate', bringing three neighbouring branches such as those at Leeds Road, Outwood and Wrenthorpe, or the ones at Kirkgate, Thornes, and Thornes Lane together under a single manager. The case was deferred until the manager could bring a list of all employees liable for military service together, with details of their medical fitness or otherwise.

It wasn't just local people who found themselves facing Wakefield's Tribunal. Ernest Saunders, described as 'a coloured man' from the West Indies, appeared before them in September 1916. He explained that he had registered himself at Lincoln as required but had taken a job as a ship's steward. His ship had later been sunk by the Germans and he had lost his documents. After returning to Britain via America he told the Tribunal that army recruiters had turned him away and his attempts to serve on a minesweeper had failed. Unsurprisingly perhaps, he had decided that 'if they wanted him, they must fetch him'. Fetch him they did, he was handed over to the military authorities. In June 1917, a young man named John Foy was arrested at Sandal for vagrancy and brought before the Military Service Tribunal. He was a farm labourer but Chief Constable T.M. Harris reported that lately Foy had been going from farm to farm begging and was out of work. Foy had with him a certificate of exemption from the Midlothian Tribunal as long as he remained in work. For once, though, the Military Representative decided not to push for him to be called up, telling them that 'being deaf and dumb the defendant was no good to the military authorities'. The Bench agreed to discharge him on the understanding that the police would find him work.

It was not only those unwilling to serve who appeared before the tribunal. In April it heard the case of an unnamed Dewsbury boot and shoe repairer who attended the Tribunal in uniform. The man had attested under the Derby Scheme but had appealed for exemption on the grounds of hardship since he would lose his business if he left for the army. When called up in February he had refused to sign the relevant papers as his appeal had not been heard. He was told by staff at the Dewsbury Recruiting Office that he had no choice and was pressured into signing on with threats of being dragged into a court martial. As a result he had signed the papers, been sent to various camps for training and, therefore, had lost his business and had not had chance to make any arrangements for closing it down properly. Since he had already lost his livelihood, the tribunal were unable to grant him exemption but urged him to seek compensation from the War Office and offered their support in his claim. In December, an Ossett rag merchant appealed against his call up after having already made three attempts to enlist. At the start of the war he had closed his business and joined the Officer Training Corps, spending around £35 before being medically rejected shortly before he was due to gain his commission. He went to Leeds but was again rejected before heading to York to try to join the artillery. Taking the hint, he had gone home and reopened his business only to be called up and passed as fit for home defence duties. By then, his enthusiasm had waned and the tribunal agreed that he had done what he could. Exemption was granted.

Those unhappy with the Military Service Tribunal decisions could ask for their case to be heard by an Appeal Tribunal. Sitting in County Hall, the East Central (West Riding) Appeal Tribunal had responsibility for the area from Slaithwaite in the West to Goole in the East and the members included Edmund Bruce (Huddersfield), Joe Haley (Dewsbury) and Edward Lancaster (Barnsley). Benjamin Littlewood (Huddersfield), Frederick Mallalieu (Delph), Edmund Stonehouse (the Mayor of Wakefield) and Ben Turner (Batley), were also members. All but Stonehouse were already local magistrates. It was their job to hear from those determined not to serve, including the case of the Castleford man who argued that his work as a book-maker was of national importance or the man who objected to killing under any circumstances, but who was known to enjoy blood sports.

One man claimed that his religion of Spiritualism prevented him from joining up whilst tripe-dressers, barbers, corset makers and others all insisted that their work was vital to the war effort. They also had to manage the difficult cases of men who claimed conscientious objection.

Contrary to popular belief, the British government had worked hard to try to accommodate those who felt unable to serve in combat. Unlike conscription in other countries, the Military Service Act allowed a man to ask for exemption on a variety of grounds, including moral and religious conscience. Conscientious objectors could ask for exemption on the basis of their beliefs and the Tribunal had to form a judgement about whether an individual had genuine grounds for claiming they were not able to serve. The *Ossett Observer* of 25 March reported on a debate in Parliament on the problems of managing conscientious objectors:

Mr Lloyd George said that tribunals had a difficult task in discriminating between the person who had a real conscientious objection and him who made use of it as a cloak for cowardice. It was clear from the evidence that some men only had a conscientious objection to being fired at. He agreed that the test applied to these cases might be improved. Questions as to whether the claimants had expressed conscientious objections before the war, or had made sacrifices for conscience, were relevant and ought to be pressed home. He had been twitted with being a conscientious objector. That was true; he held very strong views about the injustice of a certain war. What were they to do with the genuine conscientious objector? The Government were entitled to ask that every citizen should contribute something to helping the country. He had conscientious objectors in his own department who were helping him to improve the condition of workers in the workshops. They would rather be shot than fight, but they were doing valuable work which was perfectly consistent with their consciences. Surely conscientious objectors could not object to assisting the Royal Army Medical Corps. If he had been recruited in the Boer War, he would not have hesitated for a moment to take part in helping to succour the wounded. What was there inconsistent in a man, who objected to war, doing his best to cure its wounds and repair its damage? If a conscientious objector told him he objected to doing that, he said without

Those whose conscience did not allow them to enlist found little sympathy among those whose fathers, sons and brothers were already overseas.

hesitation that the real reason was not conscience but fear. Mr Walter Long was sympathetic towards genuine cases, but in plain English, he could not understand the position of a man who claimed all the rights of citizenship, who enjoyed the right to live in this country, with all its privileges and institutions, who did as he liked, it might be that he amassed a fortune under the protection of our laws, and then when every institution that we cared for was at stake, when our liberties, our privileges, it might be the lives of those we cared for most were in danger – men who claimed all these privileges and yet declined to raise a hand in defence, even of women and children. Mr Long said it was the intention of the Government to devise machinery by which the conscientious objector, when he had established his case to the satisfaction of the tribunal, would have an opportunity of doing some work for the country which would be of importance.

Lance Corporal Willett of the local KOYLI battalion, wrote home to his sister about his feelings towards the men now appearing at Tribunals back home:

The man who has hung on until it came to practically compulsion, with no reason at all, except the saving his own selfish skin, ought to be ashamed to wear the same cloth as the men who died in their countries [sic] cause in 1914. The khaki uniform is a dress of honour. These men should have a dress of their own and be forced to emigrate when the war is over. Thank God there is only a small percentage of such men in the United Kingdom. I would much rather be under a soldier's wooden cross than in their ranks any time. We have many a laugh out here when we get the papers with reports of the tribunals. I saw that one chap said he would stand by and watch his sisters be assaulted. He said he would pray to God. Much good that would do him! God helps those who help themselves. Praying did not save the Belgians at Louvain, not physically anyhow. May the Lord grant that we shall never need such men.

But the army needed them. By 1916 conscription was the only way to keep Britain in the war. The first category of conscientious objector, 'Non-combatants', were relatively easy for the Tribunals and military to manage since they were prepared to accept call-up into the army, but not to be trained to use weapons or indeed have anything to do with weapons. The British army had no precedents or guidelines for managing conscription and so tried to compromise by creating the Non-Combatant Corps, to provide a guarantee that conscientious objectors (known as 'COs' or 'Conchies') would not be asked to perform combat duties. Commanded by regular army officers and NCOs, they would be soldiers and subject to army discipline but would not be expected to fight. Instead they would be a labour force doing a variety of jobs such as building, cleaning, loading and unloading stores, other than munitions, behind the lines in Britain and overseas. Around 3,400 COs accepted postings to the Corps during the war. Equally, 'Alternativists' who objected to military service but were prepared to undertake alternative civilian employment not under any military control could be exempted on condition that they actually did this work. Alternativist James Digby, of Duke Street Castleford, for example, was exempted combatant service in June 1916 and assigned to the Non-Combatant Corps but was discharged the following March to work in the mines back in his home town.

Far more difficult was the task of deciding what to do with men from pacifist religions who had already served in France. At the beginning of the war some Quakers formed the Friends War Victims Relief Committee (FWVRC) and travelled overseas at their own expense to aid refugees forced away from their homes by the fighting, continuing the work throughout the war and its aftermath. At the same time, another group of young Quakers who were trained in first aid set up the Friends Ambulance Unit (FAU), explaining that their 'ideal as a voluntary unit is to ease pressure on overworked or inadequate staff.' Service with the FAU gave them a way to help the wounded without supporting the war itself, treating Allied and German wounded alike, although as one member later explained, 'One has to help the latter mostly by stealth, but it is lovely to be able to do so now and then'. The French army reportedly regarded the FAU as 'amiable and efficient cranks' but there is no doubt that their bravery and determination saved many lives.

The Quaker School at Ackworth recorded 192 former students had volunteered for work overseas either with the FAU or the FWVRC, but the coming of conscription brought new dilemmas and many Conscientious Objectors given exemption on condition that they served with the FAU found their position increasingly problematic. Back in 1914, some FAU workers had expressed their concern that

Anyone not in uniform faced pressure from neighbours.

they might be taking non-combatant work away from volunteer soldiers, meaning that men would be placed in danger and possibly killed because the FAU was doing tasks the soldiers would otherwise be doing. The coming of conscription meant that the men freed up for front-line service would not be volunteers who chose the army but potentially unwilling conscripts forced into the front line. Some who resigned found themselves confronted by Tribunals who wanted to use their having been in France with the FAU as evidence that they did not object to alternative compulsory service and ordered them either back into the FAU or into the Non-Combatant Corps.

Religious beliefs were respected by Tribunals but the outbreak of war had also brought a sharp rise in the number of men claiming to belong to pacifist denominations. In April 1916, for example, Flockton power-loom tuner Fred Peel was arrested by the police and charged with absconding from the military after the Appeal Tribunal's confirmation of the original decision that he must accept the call-up. He explained that he was a Christadelphian and that his faith forbade him to enlist, but he was found guilty anyway. The organisation had petitioned parliament for exemption back in February 1915, stating that their objection was based on a literal interpretation of God's command not to kill. Many, however, were quite prepared to accept well-paid work in munitions factories. This apparent inconsistency was a problem for individuals at the early tribunals, but negotiations with the Central Tribunal in April 1915 had established that Christadelphians could be granted conditional exemption dependent upon them agreeing to carrying out work of national importance. Further negotiations with the Army Council led to these men being granted a special 'Christadelphian Certificate of Exemption from Military Service' by the Army Council in August 1916. This, though, applied only to men who had been members of the church prior to the war and Peel's own father testified that Fred had joined the Christadelphians in October 1914.

Most difficult of all were 'absolutists' who claimed to be opposed to the idea of conscription itself, as well as war in general, and who presented themselves as upholders of civil liberty and the freedom of the individual. Absolutists believed that any form of alternative service supported the war effort and, in effect, supported the immoral practice of conscription as well. As a result, they refused any form of compromise on the basis that working as a postman or tram driver could release another man for duty and therefore supported the war. In one case a man who had been ordered to serve in the Non-Combatant Corps refused to muck out horse stalls at an army remount centre in Britain on the basis that the horses were destined for service in the forces, and by cleaning their stalls he would be 'directly contributing to the war'.

At a time when conscription relied on men being willing to obey the law of their country, allowing some to evade service on the basis that they did not want to go would open the floodgates for all to claim to have grounds to object. Hundreds of young men had moved to Ireland, where conscription was not enforced. There were genuine objectors among them but also large numbers of men who simply did not want to serve. Some presented absolutists as being heroes, and elaborate escape networks developed of safe houses willing to shelter men evading service, whilst others saw them as cowards hiding behind the freedoms other men were fighting and dying to protect. Some, like the man who refused Salford's Tribunal's attempts to grant him total exemption, were regarded as cranks; especially after he insisted that he must be exempted as a conscientious objector rather than because, as the Tribunal's military representative patiently pointed out, he only had one leg.

In April 1916, 30-year-old scythe stone maker George Burton of Ackworth appeared before the Wakefield Appeals Tribunal, who upheld the Military Service Tribunal's decision that he had not proved his case, but could be assigned to the Non-Combatant Corps. Once his appeal failed, Burton was legally deemed to be a serving soldier, so when, in May, he refused orders, he was brought before a court martial. A month later he was in France, where he served for the rest of the war, but again refused orders, in December 1917, and was sentenced to eighty days' hard labour. Supporters of the COs wrote of men being 'crucified' for their beliefs but whilst treatment of COs could be harsh, COs who were sent to Non-Combatant units and who refused to obey orders were treated the same as any other soldier, so when they consistently refused to obey orders they were usually given 'Field Punishment No. 1'. Introduced in 1881 following the abolition of flogging, it was a common means of dealing with military offences overseas, and the convicted man could be placed in some sort of restraints, and attached to a fixed object such as a gun wheel or a fence post for no more than 2 hours per day, three days out of every four. A Commanding Officer could award field punishment for up to twenty-eight days or a court martial for up to ninety days, depending on the severity of the crime, and the aim was to provide a clear deterrent to other potential offenders. The punishment was often applied with the arms stretched out and the legs tied together, giving rise to the nickname 'crucifixion'. Those who chose to see the COs as religious martyrs seized on the term and it is still commonly used to suggest that they were harshly treated, but one survivor, Alfred Evans, claimed that 'it was very uncomfortable, but certainly not humiliating', and in many cases conscientious objectors even saw 'F.P. No. 1' as a badge of honour.

In one extreme case, in June 1916, thirty-four COs who had refused to obey orders in France were court martialed and sentenced to death. This was not because they were conscientious objectors – after all their appeals had failed – but because they were legally serving soldiers and, like every other soldier, subject to military law. Military law in wartime is by necessity harsh, and the generals had to consider what message it would send to other troops if they allowed some to pick and choose what orders to obey. Only after a pause did the officer then tell them that General Haig had commuted the sentence to ten years' imprisonment, which would be served in England. Ignoring the open disobedience of the COs could have had disastrous consequences at a time when the army was preparing for the huge Somme offensive, and even sentencing them to ten years imprisonment risked signalling to men in front-line trenches that they could escape to a nice safe prison cell far behind the lines or even back home in England, by refusing to do their duty, but political sensitivities around conscription saved them. On their return, the men were sent to civilian prisons to serve out their sentences.

By the middle of 1916, there were around 6,000 COs under some form of military control and such was the scale of indiscipline that Kitchener recommended to the Cabinet that the government should establish a civilian organisation to employ them 'under conditions as severe as those of soldiers at the front', under what would become known as 'equal sacrifice' principle. At the end of May, a new Army Order was drafted, which directed that CO's convicted by court martial of offences against discipline, and who had been sentenced to a term of imprisonment, should be held at the nearest civil prison. It was also proposed that these men should not be discharged from the army, but instead placed in Class W of the Army Reserve as 'soldiers whose service is deemed to be valuable to the country in civil rather than military employment'. In effect this meant that those who accepted work under the Home Office Scheme, but breached its conditions, could be recalled by the army and made subject to court martial again, if appropriate, and returned, on sentence, to a civil

Prison staff at Wakefield Prison. In 1916 the remaining prisoners were moved out and the locks removed so it could accommodate conscientious objectors.

prison. In order to manage these cases, prisons at Warwick and Wakefield were emptied of their usual inmates and converted into 'Work Centres'.

A Home Office scheme was created under which COs who were serving sentences in civilian prisons, including those sent back from the army in France, could have their prison sentences suspended provided they were willing to work. By October 1916, the prison had been emptied and its cell locks removed to create Wakefield Work Centre where COs wore civilian clothes and were paid 8d per day to undertake work under the same conditions as local civilians. The Centre was run by a manager, not a governor, and COs could elect committees to make representations to the management, create social and sports clubs and outside working hours and every Sunday, they were free to go outside as they wished. Despite the relaxed regime, several of the men threatened with execution in France in May had to be transferred from Wakefield to the prison at Armley, in Leeds, in December after refusing to comply with the terms of their agreement.

Feelings toward the COs were mixed. The *Yorkshire Evening Post* of 18 May 1918 reported on events in Knutsford where 'disturbances' outside the prison housing COs had led local authorities to approach the Home Office to have them moved: 'It was made clear that the presence of the "Conchies" was repulsive to the population and a menace to peace, and it was highly desirable that they should be sent to a more populous district where they would be less conspicuous if no less obnoxious. They hoped Knutsford would soon be rid of the nuisance. The announcement was received with delight by residents and wounded soldiers who crowded the court. They rose en masse and cheered lustily'. By contrast, in October the same year, the *Derby Telegraph* reported on the local Labour Party's resolution expressing its 'admiration of the consistency and courage with which the absolutist conscientious objectors at Wakefield have maintained their stand for liberty of conscience'.

By then the regime at Wakefield had changed. The relaxed regime had led to a bizarre situation where men on the run from the law had hidden out in the prison without being noticed, in some cases for months. More and more wounded ex-servicemen had been employed to act as wardens to bring things under control. Food shortages meant that rations had been reduced to 8 ounces of bread per day and only 12 ounces of bully beef per week, supplemented from time to time by tinned salmon. For most workers, rations were basic, but for those employed on foundry work, it was barely enough. Despite the hardships, though, the COs were reported to be continuing to stage plays and concerts.

When the Knutsford contingent transferred into Wakefield, they arrived as tensions between the COs and locals were reaching breaking point. For some time groups of discharged soldiers and other locals had taken to gathering outside the prison gates to jeer at the COs as they came and went. 'There have been wild and disorderly scenes at night along the misnamed Love Lane which leads to the portals of the gaol,' reported the *Yorkshire Evening Post* of 23 May, 'and as a result a good few of the men are in the prison hospital nursing broken heads and bruised bodies'. Prisoners had been allowed out between 5.30 and 9.30pm, and so gangs were able to lie in wait on the evening of 20 May. The trigger was never identified but several COs had their bicycles and other items stolen and one was thrown repeatedly into the beck at the rear of the prison. Some took refuge in the police station and had to be escorted back, others hid at friends' homes but were tracked down and beaten. In some cases, COs only managed to get back into the prison by climbing ladders to get over the wall – effectively having to stage a prison break-in. Sister paper the *Yorkshire Post* described this as a 'far from complimentary reception' but noted 'some of the burly young objectors, though professedly opposed to fighting, not having objected to give battle'.

By 1918, the country was ever more desperate for recruits and the Wakefield Tribunal spent much of its time considering appeals from the National Service representative against exemptions already made. So serious was the problem that he personally spent time at the Wakefield Employment Exchange looking for candidates to replace those seeking exemption. The battle with the Wakefield Tramways Company continued, with a debate about retaining male inspectors, when women had shown they were clearly able to do the job. In June, the Tramways Company applied for exemption for a 44-year-old driver. The man had eight children aged between 18 months and 20 years and averaged 68 hours a week working for the company, including training one-legged discharged soldiers to drive the trams. Additionally, he worked 24 hours a week for a market gardener and cared for two vegetable allotments of his own. He was given six months' exemption and freed from the customary obligation to train with the Volunteer Corps. By the time his months of grace were up, the war had ended.

Tensions continued long after the war. COs began be released from prison by mid 1919 but this meant in some cases they were back home before men conscripted at the same time. Some had been broken in health during their time in prison, others had suffered psychologically. In November 1917, CO John Taylor attempted to slash his own throat with a razor and was committed to the Wakefield Asylum after medical treatment. He died there in January, but the authorities concluded that neither the military nor the prison was to blame, saying that his mental health had suffered as a result of air raids near his home in London.

In achieving their aim of opposing the war, some COs had also achieved the government's aim that they should make an 'equal sacrifice'. Their sentences meant they were denied a vote until 1926, but to many that seemed a small price to pay when the streets were full of bereaved families and disabled men. In some places they were shunned and refused jobs, in others treated as heroes and elected to government positions, but the animosity felt by those who had served for those they felt had accepted the benefits without any of the costs would survive for many years.

CHAPTER 5

News from the Front

The first weeks of the war were marked by massive public interest but very little real information about what was actually happening. In the absence of hard news, the public turned instead to a flood of stories based on half truths, rumours and even pure fiction. Propaganda efforts to portray the enemy as brutish 'Huns' began immediately.

Forty years earlier, during the Franco-Prussian War of 1870–71, the Germans had suffered casualties at the hands of civilian *franc-tireurs* who wore no uniform as they shot at Germans far behind the front lines. The laws of war offered no protection to them and they could be executed if captured. In 1914, stories emerged of German troops in Belgium shooting boy scouts and were presented as though they were murdering young boys, but pictures also appeared in newspapers of teens in Scout uniform openly carrying their own rifles as they marched alongside soldiers. Even British soldiers in France accepted that the shooting of spies, *franc-tireurs* and obstructive local officials was both widespread and legitimate.

The sacking of the Belgian town of Louvain between 26 and 30 August came as retaliation for actions by *franc-tireurs* during a counter-attack by Belgian forces, which had caused a panic among German troops. As an official German source at the time explained, the 'only means of preventing surprise attacks from the civil population has been to interfere with unrelenting severity and to create examples which, by their frightfulness, would be a warning to the entire country'. Meanwhile, in Germany, almost identical rumours spread of the savage treatment of civilians in East Prussia by invading Russians whilst in the German army; wild tales of the torture and murder of wounded Germans by Belgian women and children fuelled the anger with which troops responded to real or imagined attacks by *franc-tireurs*. All sides, it seemed, were determined to portray the enemy as sub-human barbarians.

Terrible as the genuine atrocities like Louvain were, the British public were ever eager for more. At all levels of society, pornographic stories about the rape, torture and murder of women and children in Belgium circulated and were accepted without question. Lord Bryce, former Regius Professor of Civil Law at Oxford, Professor of Juris-prudence at Manchester and a historian respected for his work on the Holy Roman Empire, was commissioned to investigate 'Alleged German Outrages', and his report, published in 1915, was based on 1,200 unsworn depositions from unidentified Belgian refugees. None of the committee actually interviewed any of the supposed witnesses themselves and hearsay evidence was accepted as fact. Bryce himself was aware even before the report was published that much of what was in it was unreliable but the government hoped that his reputation as a scholar would make up for any concerns about the actual con-tent, and the report was widely circulated and quoted in American newspapers.

In Britain Lord Northcliffe, owner of the best selling *Daily Mail*, had offered £200 for any genuine photograph of a mutilated refugee, but the prize was never claimed and American correspondent William Shepherd of United Press later recalled: 'I was in Belgium when the first atrocity stories went out. I hunted and hunted for atrocities during the first days of the atrocity scare. I couldn't find atrocities. I couldn't find people who had seen them. I travelled on trains with Belgians who had fled from the German lines and I spent much time amongst Belgian refugees. I offered sums of money for photographs of children whose hands had been cut off or who had been wounded or injured in other ways. I never found a first-hand Belgian atrocity story; and when I ran down second-hand stories they all petered out.'

The story of a Scottish nurse from Dumfries, 23-year-old Grace Hume, was widely reported. Under headlines of 'fiendish attack on Scottish nurse', 'fiendish brutality' and 'Germans mutilate Scottish nurse', they told of how nurse Hume had left home to help in a Belgian hospital at the start of the war. By September she was said to have carried a wounded man from the battlefield, shooting a German soldier dead as he tried to stop her. On 6 September, it was reported that German troops had overrun her hospital and embarked on a rampage, murdering and beheading the wounded men. When nurse Hume attempted to defend her patients, she was tortured and her breasts cut off before they left her to die in agony. A second nurse named Millard wrote of how Hume had shot a German who attacked her patients and for almost two weeks the story ran in several papers until *The Times* revealed that not only did Nurse Millard not exist, but that Grace Hume had never left the country and was, in fact, working in Huddersfield. The whole story had been made up by her 17-year-old sister, Kate, who made headlines herself when she was arrested for the hoax.

At the end of August, the *Hull Daily Mail* reported that 'a very curious and persistent rumour has been circulated in Hull, coming from numerous very reliable people, none of whom, however, have it at first hand, that bodies of Russian troops have landed in Scotland for the purpose of proceeding to Belgium . . .'. The story quickly took on its own momentum around the entire country. Almost 200 trains full of Russians had passed through York. A Scottish landowner boasted that 125,000 Cossacks had crossed his land. The *Daily Mail* quoted a reliable source who claimed a million Russians had travelled through Stroud in a single night. Reverend Andrew Clark, of Great Leighs, in Essex, recorded in his diary that there was a report 'current in Braintree – that a Russian force has been brought to Yorkshire and landed there: and that the East Coast trains have been commandeered to transport them rapidly south en route for the French theatre of war . . .'. He also noted how a magistrate friend had told him 'that an old servant of his had written that from her bedroom window she had watched train after train for hours, passing by night to Bristol. There were no lights in the carriages, but by the light of the cigars and cigarettes they were smoking, the black beards of the Russians could be seen. . .'.

Reverend Clark did not feel the need to question just how bright the cigarettes must have been for an elderly servant to be able to make out the smoker's beard on a darkened train at some distance and in the middle of the night, but as the story grew, 'witnesses' told their incredulous audiences how the Russians, after days aboard ships from Archangel and long journeys on trains in the heat of an English summer, had boarded ships at the Channel ports with snow still on their boots. No matter how far fetched the story might seem when the facts were examined, there were always at least a few people willing to believe it and pass it on. Finally, after weeks of speculation, the Under Secretary of State for War, Harold Tennant, was forced to explain to the House of Commons that 'I am uncertain whether it will gratify or displease my honourable friend to learn that no Russian troops have been conveyed through Great Britain to the Western Front area of the European War.'

On 29 September 1914, Welsh author Arthur Machen published a short story entitled 'The Bowmen' in the *London Evening News* inspired by accounts that he had read of the fighting at Mons and an idea he had had soon after the battle. Machen had already written a number of factual articles on the war and set his story at the time of the retreat from the Battle of Mons in August, describing how phantom bowmen from the Battle of Agincourt had appeared after a British soldier called on St George to help his unit survive a German attack. It was written from the view of the soldier himself and seemed as though it was an actual report. Unfortunately, the paper did not say the story was fiction and ran another short fiction piece in the same edition. Machen was soon approached by people asking for more details and requests to reprint the story in parish magazines. Machen made it clear that the story was completely made up but one priest told him that he was mistaken, the 'facts' of the story must be true and all Machen had done was to elaborate on a real account. As Machen later said: 'It seemed that my light fiction had been accepted by the congregation of this particular church as the solidest of facts; and it was then that it began to dawn on me that if I had failed in the art of letters, I had succeeded, unwittingly, in the art of deceit. This happened, I should think, some time in April, and the snowball of rumour that was then set rolling has been rolling ever since, growing bigger and bigger, till it is now swollen to a monstrous size.'

In the following months, more and more accounts of the 'Angels of Mons' appeared and more details were added, including reports of Germans found dead with arrow wounds on their bodies. Despite Machen's best efforts, the story took on a life of its own. Reverend Boddy, of Sunderland, spent two months travelling around France and reported that 'the evidence, though not always direct, is remarkably cumulative and came through channels which were entitled to respect'. These channels were always what modern folklorists call 'a friend of a friend' – an unnamed nurse at an unspecified military hospital was treating an unidentified soldier when she heard the story. 'Eyewitness' accounts were published using letters from soldiers who had not even been in France at the time the events were claimed to have happened and Mr Blackburn of Keighley appealed for accounts by men who were at Mons to send their stories of the angels to him 'as this vision surely could not have been invented'. Machen would spend the rest of his career trying to get people to believe him when he said he had made it up.

The real news from France was less encouraging. The tiny British army was in full retreat and in very real danger of being overwhelmed by the German onslaught. On Monday, 24 August, the day after the disaster at Mons, Lord Kitchener, Secretary of State for War, visited Winston Churchill, then First Lord of the Admiralty. As the two men most responsible for Britain's defence, they read an alarming telegram from the commander of the British Expeditionary Force, General French. He reported that the heavily fortified Belgian city of Namur – the key to defending Belgium – had fallen, a general retreat had been ordered and in French's opinion 'immediate attention should be directed to the defence of Le Havre.' The Allies were supposed to be halting the German advance at the French border; Le Havre was 210 miles away on the French coast. It looked as though a disaster was unfolding.

The Times of Wednesday, 26 August, reported that 'the Allies have fallen back, but their resistance has cost Germany very dear. The battle has begun; yet its first days rank it, according to past standards, as one of the greatest in its history.' But, it warned, 'their losses have been considerable. They are estimated by the Field Marshal in command at over 2,000. No details have yet been received.' The next day, it told readers there was little information available about the great battle going on in France: 'Though we know that the British Army acquitted itself with distinction at Mons, we still know very little more. Even the casualty lists are not yet made public.'

On Friday, a report from Rouen described the arrival of the wounded: 'These were not the worst of the wounded, for the worst cases are still up country. Some had only bad feet, broken by heavy marching; others had bullet or shrapnel wounds in feet, or hands or head; a small percentage of the 500 had the stomach wounds which every seasoned soldier dreads; only one went through the pains of death upon the station.'

The authorities were not keen that the public should read that sort of account so the arrival of the wounded in Britain was brief and to the point. 'Special trains were in readiness at the quayside, and the men, it is believed, were hurried away to [the large military hospital at] Netley. The public were excluded from the docks and the greatest secrecy was maintained.' Such secrecy did nothing to inspire public confidence. In Whitehall, politicians argued about how much people should be told. Some argued that releasing the truth about the retreat in France would be bad for morale but others thought that it could be used to encourage recruiting by making the public aware of the increasingly real possibility of an invasion. As one put it, 'the time is past when a great and free and enlightened democracy can go to war in the dark'.

By Saturday, *The Times* explained: 'Our soldiers have fought as men of the British race have ever fought, but it would serve no useful purpose now to hide the heaviness of the price of their bravery.' The next day, a special edition broke with tradition by putting a news story on the front page, under the headline 'Fiercest Fight in History: Heavy Losses of British Troops', it presented the latest war news as passed by the government's press censors. A sub-heading of 'Broken British Regiments' spoke of 'a bitter tale' of a 'retreating and broken army ... battered with marching', and of 'grievously injured regiments', with nearly all their officers lost. It caused an immediate uproar with the paper accused of being irresponsible and sensationalist with a more positive version quickly being sent out to newspapers by government sources, but the story was out. As some had noted, it had the potential to act as a powerful recruiting agent. On Wednesday, 2 September, *The Times* noted, 'The men of London and the Provinces have evidently realised since Sunday that the success of Great Britain and her Allies against Germany can only be ensured by large additions to the British forces in the field. No one doubted that as soon as this was really understood recruits would come forward in abundance. Monday saw more men joining the colours than any day since the war began, and yesterday easily eclipsed Monday's record.' In the six days between 30 August and 5 September 174,901 men enlisted compared with 100,000 who had done so in the three weeks between the 4th and the 22nd of August.

One way of getting around censorship and reporting the war was by publishing stories about letters received from local men on active service to add colour to the bland official communiques. Many of these letters, originally intended only for the reader, were hardly calculated to ease the fears of families at home and spoke openly of death and discomfort but they were eagerly read by civilians trying to find out what was going on. In 1914, the Post Office was the biggest single employer in the world with over 250,000 staff handling an estimated 6 billion items of mail per year as well as the telephone system and running branch post offices and savings banks. Soon after war broke out, it had lost around 11,000 staff to the forces as reservists went back to their units. Supported by union leaders, Post Office management sent every male employee a letter encouraging him to enlist and by December 1914 28,000 had done so. Although services were reduced as a result, it remained a very busy organisation.

A special Army Postal Service staffed by former Post Office employees operated to manage mail to and from those serving overseas and to maintain communications between front line units and in the weeks before Christmas 1917, around 19,000 mailbags – approximately 1 million letters – crossed the Channel every day. By the end of 1914, the London Home Depot covered 5 acres and was said to be the biggest wooden building in the world. In all, its staff of 2,500 women had processed around 2 billion letters and 114 million parcels destined for the forces. The static nature of the war meant that a network of deliveries could be set up that meant a letter from Wakefield could often reach someone in a front line trench faster than a letter could be sent to a civilian in the UK.

A 'quick firer' from France.

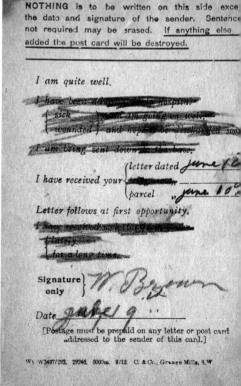

A postcard home from France. Note the censor has scratched out the name of the cathedral.

As a result, soldiers were able to write home regularly, but for many, letter writing was a new art. For those who found it difficult or had no time to write, Army Form A2042, the Field Service Postcard, was available and known to the men as a 'quick firer'. Other than the address and the man's name, nothing could be added to the postcard, which was pre-printed with a few sentences about his health and whether he had received mail from home. All the man had to do was cross out the bits that didn't apply. Behind the lines, ordinary tourist postcards were available and later special wartime cards showing battle-damaged tourist attractions were sold by French civilians or through service canteens at base camps. Enterprising photographers produced portrait postcards and a soldier's war service could be documented by a series of these postcards. More elaborate embroidered silk cards were also available, often showing the regimental badge or patriotic messages. Longer letters were supposed to be read and censored by the man's officer before they could be posted but a special green envelope was available for more personal mail. To avoid the embarrassment of having his officer read personal letters to his wife or sweetheart a soldier could sometimes get hold of the special envelope and sign a declaration that it contained no information about military matters. It might still be censored at a base camp to the rear but would generally pass through unhindered.

At home, censorship meant that there was little in the way of real news about the war but editors quickly found that reporting on the arrival of letters from the front allowed them to get around the restrictions. Soon, family, friends and employers began bringing letters in so that a short story could be put together about it or, if several letters had been received, it was possible to piece together some idea of what was really going on.

One of the first letters from the front appeared in the *Wakefield Express* on 12 September when George Woodhead wrote to his wife at Portobello Road. George was serving aboard HMS *Crecy* when it took on German prisoners following the sinking of the German light cruiser SMS *Mainz* in the first naval battle of the war, at Heligoland Bight. In the letter he explained that as he understood it, the crew of the German ship had been in a state of mutiny and that its captain and officers had begun shooting their own men, claiming that the prisoners had not eaten for several days and were desperately in need of food. Given that the *Mainz* had single-handedly fought a British fleet of four cruisers and six destroyers for almost 2 hours, inflicting heavy damage on several British ships until one by one the German guns were blasted away and the ship sunk by torpedoes, the suggestion that they were near mutiny seems a bit unlikely and prompted perhaps more by the general propaganda being spread about an easy victory than the reality of the situation.

More letters appeared from other local men. In October, motor engineer Walter Judge received letters from three of his employees who had gone out to France with the first of the BEF. Foreman F.H. Harris wrote that 'I don't think that up to last night I had twelve hours sleep in five days. The worst of it is that we have had a lot of rain and no change of clothes ... I have been talking to a German officer who, along with thirty of his men, have been taken prisoners and I can tell you that they are very glad to be prisoners. This officer, who had eight wounds, could talk good English.' In November 1914, Private Frank Barnes, a Sheffield man serving with the 2nd Battalion, Warwickshire Regiment, wrote home. His unit had been involved in hard fighting and he described the shock of finding British soldiers

Gunner Alfred Gravett of the Royal Garrison Artillery kept a record of his war service through the postcards he sent to his sister in Plumpton, showing his progress through training and out to France with his group of friends. It even included cards produced when he was wounded. (*Courtesy of Richard Knowles*)

From Gunner Gravett's collection of souvenir postcards, an image of his mates in training. (*Courtesy of Richard Knowles*)

who had been murdered after surrendering during the retreat from Mons. His unit counter-attacked to take their objective at bayonet point. He was amongst those detailed to round up any remaining enemy: 'Presently I got another shock. I was standing near a party of fifteen Germans when all at once one turned round and said in excellent English: "Excuse me, but is there anyone here who comes

Mates of Gunner Gravett pose for a studio portrait before deployment overseas (*Courtesy of Richard Knowles*)

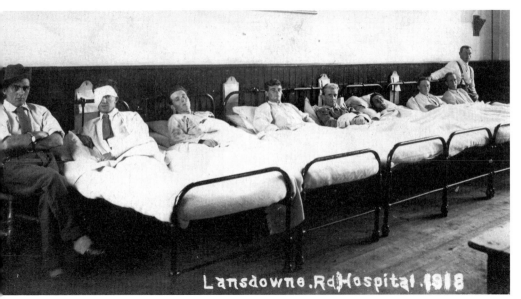

Even being wounded was cause for a souvenir picture. (*Courtesy of Richard Knowles*)

from Sheffield?" Well, you can fancy how I felt, as I was the only man from Sheffield as all the other chaps came from Brum. After I had recovered my breath I got into conversation with him. He was not so old, and told me as much about Sheffield as I knew myself. "Damned fighting", he said, "let me get back to England and my wife and children. I have been trying to get captured for several days and have only just succeeded".'

As the first Christmas of the war approached, a great deal of effort was made to ensure that every Wakefield man serving in the forces received a gift of some description. The retreat from Mons had seen hundreds of British soldiers taken prisoner and a Wakefield Prisoner of War Fund was established with its headquarters in the home of Canon Richard Phipps, the Wakefield Diocesan Secretary, and his wife at Manygates House. By October 1915, Mrs Phipps had recruited thirty-three Wakefield women who each maintained contact with one of the men held at Doberitz Camp in Germany. Pupils at Wakefield Girls High School provided parcels for twelve further men and another twelve were catered for directly from the Fund. Most of the men were members of KOYLI, the Duke of Wellington's Yorkshire Regiment or the Royal Navy. According to the *Wakefield Express*, Thomas Parkes of the Royal Navy wrote to Mrs Phipps to thank the organisation for gifts of foodstuffs, shirts, scarves and tobacco and Private J. Mason, KOYLI, reported in a letter that he had received three parcels from the Mayoress, Mrs Stonehouse. Working with General Sir A. Wynne, the KOYLI Prisoner of War Secretary, by

September 1916 the group was in a position to send each known prisoner from Wakefield a complete set of outer clothing and two sets of under garments. Bread was supplied twice weekly from Switzerland and each man received a weekly food parcel worth 4s. Letters to and from prisoners of war passed through neutral countries and a similar arrangement was in place for the men held in Lofthouse Park.

When the time came for the Wakefield men of the KOYLI to go to France in April 1915, sharing letters home became a way of keeping family, friends and neighbours informed about what was going on and at first it seemed as though they were having fun. Sergeant Herbert Henson was in charge of two machine-guns and in his first letter home he described the scene: 'They call them trenches but they are more like forts it consists of sandbags making a parapet 6ft high above the level of the ground and behind are the dugouts. The dugouts are like a little colony of huts they consist of earthwork and sandbags about 3ft high with a roof of corrugated iron on top and earth ... We had four gun emplacements about 100 yards apart or so covered over from areoplane [sic] observation they were quite alright ... We have six men per gun and out of that we had to provide a sentry through the daytime and night time 2 men on duty and 1 sentry. I have had about a couple of hours sleep each night and get the rest during the daytime when I got the chance ... We mount the gun

British PoWs were able to write home via the Red Cross and would receive letters and parcels from home.

nearly on the parapet when it gets dark and keep a sharp look out for working parties and then you let them have it and by Jove they don't half cuss and shout.'

A series of letters to the *Wakefield Express* described what can only be described as slanging matches between the front line trenches as both sides traded insults. German soldiers shouted 'England no good' and at one point 'asked us when our navy was coming out and when we were going to give it up and give in.' 'Of course a suitable reply was given', noted Captain Clayton-Smith. Some, conscious of the worry their families were coping with, kept their messages short and positive: 'We are all as happy as can be and are making the best of everything', wrote G.M. Thurlwell to his parents in Pontefract. Others were less concerned about how the people at home might be feeling: 'We have done very well up to now,' wrote Private Wood, ' having had only one killed and seven wounded in our regiment. I am very pleased to say I am safe and sound yet, and I hope to keep so, but all the same it is hell upon earth. We are short of nothing out here only cigs and I now you will send me some'.

Meanwhile, as the KOYLI men settled into trench routine, news of one of Wakefield's more unusual war casualties came when Gunner H. Boldy, of Wakefield Battery RFA, was on guard duty outside the Battery's headquarters in the town, on 7 May 1915 when lightning struck a nearby chimney stack and the blast knocked him to the ground. 'Dazed and stunned' he was taken to his home in Dunbar Street to recover. It was not the sort of thing that military protocols accounted for and his exact status as a war casualty is unclear. In a letter written to his family Second Lieutenant Chadwick, 1/4 KOYLI, described his first impressions of the front: 'Its wonderful how accustomed you get to bullets flying all around; of course when one comes uncommonly close it makes one wonder what would have happened if it had been still closer. It is now six days since I had my clothes off and I expect another twelve days will still see the same clothes on. We have a wonderful good cook. I think he was employed at Hagenbacks [*sic*] in Wakefield and he makes us some topping stuff. The peasants here still continue working about 2 miles behind our lines, in most cases their houses are smashed up a good bit. The houses near the firing line are simply in ruins in most cases.' For most soldiers, arrival at the front was something of an anti-climax. It was extremely rare to catch a glimpse of a German and the view from the trenches was of a seemingly empty battlefield. As a result, they often felt they had

A soldier writes home from the trenches.

nothing of any real interest to report but if letters home might have been brief, the men relished the ordinary, routine gossip of life at home and their mail is full of requests for information about family and friends.

Even as the war progressed, letters home remained largely positive. Having been in reserve during the first day of the Battle of the Somme, 1/4 and 1/5 KOYLI were ordered into the Thiepval area on the night of 2 July to take over from the badly hit Ulster Division who had been fighting hard after their attack on the first day of the battle. Thiepval Wood, where the front line trenches were positioned, was full of dead, dying and wounded men, blasted trees and discarded equipment. Veterans reported a 'wailing' noise made up of the cries of the wounded and moans of delirious and shocked men. The following morning, a 2-hour barrage of tear gas, high explosive and shrapnel shells rained down on them as they prepared to attack on German lines around the infamous Schwaben Redoubt. Throughout July, the attacks continued. Yet despite mounting losses, the mood among the Wakefield territorials remained one of optimism and determination. In a letter to his mother, written on the last day of that month, Lieutenant Chadwick told her that in the heat of summer they were plagued by mosquitoes, to add to all the other discomforts. 'Haven't had clothes off for two weeks [and] things are becoming quite lively. Will you please send me out some scent, the extraordinary mixture of odours in the trenches is becoming almost unbearable.' During August and September, he wrote separately to his mother and father. To his mother he wrote: 'I cannot express in words the extraordinary bravery and wonderful endurance of the men. There is one great consolation at these times, that is, the excellent example of the fellows that have gone.' The next day's letter went to his father: 'How many homes in England must have been darkened during the last few weeks. Oh! But it is a glorious thing. Men going to certain death with a smile on their faces, the only thought being for those at home. England has something to be justly proud of.' In September he wrote again to his father: 'One sees the finest examples of self sacrifice. Men and officers walking out to what appears absolutely certain death without a word of dissent.'

It would be easy to dismiss Lieutenant Chadwick's letters as boyish enthusiasm but Fred Cocker, a private in the same battalion who would be commissioned the following year, wrote home to his wife saying '. . . you at home see the tragedy of events in a much different sense to us out here. We don't see the weeping bereaved broken hearts out here. Men come and go for ever, and the only expression of grief which is exhibited by any one, is summed up in a remark which I heard the other day by a man who had just lost his best pal – with a look of fierce rage he broke out – "sithee! The first blank blanking german 'at ah catch' od on ah'll murder' im by inches, ah'll ..." then followed such a harrowing description of slow torture as would put hero or Kaiser into shade!'

But if Fred Cocker and his mates were spared the 'weeping bereaved broken hearts', people at home were not. Margaret Furniss, aged 15, worked for the Post Office delivering telegrams. 'We used to go to the houses with mostly distress telegrams, you know, people whose lads had got killed or injured or something like that and it was a bit distressing then ... the neighbours and that would stand in groups and as soon as they saw you of course your uniform was enough to set them off ... they'd say "oh a telegram girl" and then hang around to see what it was like and then more often than not the person you'd taken it to would be too nervous to open it and she would ask you to open it for her. If it was that someone had got wounded they'd burst out crying and you came away and left them with the neighbours.' After delivering sometimes devastating news and watching wives and mothers collapse in grief, telegram girls were expected to ask, 'will there be any reply?' Day after day they made their deliveries to Wakefield homes.

Sometime after the telegram would come a letter from the man's officer to add a few more details. The family of Bombardier Richard Goodall, from Thornes, received one such from his commanding officer, Major Clarke, to explain that during a heavy bombardment, their son had got out of the trench to help repair a vital telephone wire that had been cut. 'Death was almost instantaneous', he told them, 'and he could have suffered no pain. We buried him that evening. The officers, non-commissioned officers and men wish to convey their sincere sympathies to his parents. We all mourn his loss. He was a right good man, reliable and trustworthy and I extremely regret such a promising career should have been cut short.' As time wore on, the letters all followed the same format. He was shot through the head or heart and died quickly and without pain. A message of sympathy and a few kind words about the man. It's difficult to imagine how a young officer could write anything more.

In some cases the letter was more personal. George Lockwood, aged 22, of Edward Street, had been a student, and briefly a Sunday School teacher, was a private in the Territorials when war broke out. He went out to France with them in April 1915 and returned to England in January 1917, for training as an officer. Commissioned as a Second Lieutenant, he was posted back to France in July 1917, was gassed in August and had been back in the line only two days when he was hit again. He died of wounds at a hospital in Rouen on 3 November. His parents, George and Mary Ann, received a letter from Captain Holdstock, who explained that George had been 'wounded on the afternoon of 25th inst. It is the circumstances under which he was hit that prompt me to write. We were in a nasty part of the line, and quite isolated, and had lost half our company coming up. We had no water and in an endeavour to get some I sent four men to B[attalion] H[ead] Q[uarters]. Your son and I were sharing a frugal meal when word came that two of the men had been sniped and were unable to get back. Your son did not wait a minute, but took off his equipment and went to their rescue. He had just reached his men when he too was hit through the right arm and stomach. He was brought in by a private of the Durham Light Infantry. When I arrived at the spot he was in the trench. I bound him up and although in great pain he behaved like the hero he had already proved himself to be. I stayed with him until dusk and then got him away. You may be proud of your son. I recommended him for the Military Cross, but of course I cannot say if he will get it.'

Often, when a man died of his wounds, nurses would write from the hospitals to tell the families about his last days. Sometimes, there would be other letters from friends who had been with the man when he died, adding their condolences. Men on leave often spent much of their time visiting families on behalf of their mates. In the aftermath of a large battle, coming home on leave could be a painful experience. 'It was a harrowing time for me,' Douglas Cattell remembered, 'with the mothers of my friends asking for information about their sons. When I told them they had been killed or were missing they wouldn't believe me. In fact in some cases it cost friendships.'

Later still for families like the Lockwoods there would be more mail. Their son's effects and back pay were forwarded to them and, when the war was over, another letter came. For several years after 1919, Army Form W.5080 was sent out to the next of kin named on a deceased serviceman's records. It contained a pre-paid printed form and instructions on how to fold and return it along with a message. 'In order that I may be enabled to dispose of the plaque and scroll in commemoration of the soldier named overleaf in accordance with the wishes of His Majesty the King, I have to request that the requisite information regarding the soldier's relatives now living may be

The 'Dead Man's Penny' sent to the next of kin of those who died. The blank rectangle would contain the name of the fallen.

furnished on the form overleaf in strict accordance with the instructions printed thereon. The declaration thereon should be signed in your own handwriting and the form should be returned to me when certified by a Minister or Magistrate.' Once completed and countersigned by a minister or magistrate, the form could be returned.

Later, a commemorative scroll arrived bearing the words: 'He whom this scroll commemorates was numbered among those who, at the call of King and Country, left all that was dear to them endured hardness, faced danger, and finally passed out of the sight of men by the path of duty and self sacrifice, giving up their own lives that others might live in freedom. Let those who come after see to it that his name be not forgotten.' Later still, a large white envelope marked

'On His Majesty's Service', with a printed 'Official Paid' stamp arrived. Inside was another white envelope with the Royal Crest embossed on the reverse containing a brief letter:

Buckingham Palace
I join my grateful people in sending you this memorial of a brave life given for others in the Great War.
King George V

Inside the outer envelope was a cardboard envelope which protected a small bronze plaque with the name of the lost man. It would soon become known as the dead man's penny. Finally, in 1922, yet another package arrived at the Lockwood's home. In it were the British War Medal and the Allied Victory Medal their son had earned to go alongside the 1914/15 Star he would never wear.

CHAPTER 6

They Also Serve

The Gorgeous Wrecks

Many hundreds of thousands of men volunteered for the army in the late summer and autumn of 1914, completely swamping the recruit training system. Spoilt for choice, the army raised its minimum height standards to try to reduce the numbers coming forward. Medical standards, often ignored in the initial rush, began to be enforced more carefully, excluding men who had a stammer on the grounds that they would not be able to pass messages along in the trenches, and those with bad teeth on the basis that they would not be able to chew the hard tack ration biscuits. Truly determined men had their teeth removed so they would qualify for army issue dentures but there were many would be soldiers sent home as unfit for service. Others, men who were running small businesses or had too many dependants to rely on the painfully small separation allowances on offer to support families left behind, began to look for other ways to serve their country.

Earlier in the year, Ireland had come close to civil war over the issue of Home Rule and for some time both sides had been preparing to fight. In January 1913, the paramilitary Ulster Volunteer Force had been formed to oppose Irish self governance, soon followed by the Irish Volunteers to support it. Seeing a chance to destabilise Britain, Germany had supplied arms to both sides. In April, 24,000 rifles had been landed at Larne by the Ulster Volunteers. In June, author Erskine Childers, whose book *The Riddle of the Sands*, had told of a secret German plan to invade England, landed 900 Mauser rifles from his private yacht to support the Irish Nationalist cause, and in July newspapers around the world had shown pictures of citizen armies on both sides openly parading their weapons in shows of strength. When war broke out, fears of an uprising by German agents or a Zeppelin-led invasion were high. With the army heading for France and the Territorials seemed set to follow them, people began to fear what

PRIVATE.
Original Pattern.)

OFFICER.
(The Rank Mark is that of a
Company Commander.)

PRIVATE.
(Permissible Alternative Style.)

Volunteer Training Corps uniforms had to be of green twill, not khaki, and had to be paid for by each recruit.

would happen when the soldiers left. Inspired by what was happening in Ireland, Percy Harris wrote to *The Times* on 6 August to propose setting up a citizen's militia to defend London if the need arose. Just four days later, a group of self-appointed officers began recruiting for the London Defence Force.

In much the same way as the Boy Scout movement had taken off since 1908 by encouraging youngsters to form their own troops, the idea of a citizen army quickly took off in almost every town and city. In Swansea, 500 dockers formed a unit to guard food warehouses against looters, whilst units with titles like the National Association of Local Government Officers Special Battalion, the Businessmen's Friends Battalion, the Chief Constable's Citizen Corps and the Athlete's Volunteer Force, sprang up to learn the basics of military training using local rifle clubs and either borrowing drill instructors from the local police or paying ex-soldiers to lead the group. Armed with a variety of ancient rifles, shotguns or any other weapon they could find, they were a cause for alarm in government circles where the idea of bands of untrained armed civilians roaming the streets at a time when everyone believed that an uprising of immigrant agents could happen at any time made for a potentially dangerous scenario. Even if the Germans did come, the bands were more likely to hinder than help. They would not be covered by the Geneva Convention and could be shot out of hand as many 'terrorists' had been by the Germans during their advance through Belgium.

Despite official discouragement, the movement flourished and in November, the Central Association of Volunteer Training Corps was established with the aim of at least trying to organise the estimated 1400 groups of volunteers into some sort of manageable force. Rules were laid down around who could join to ensure no-one tried to use membership as an excuse not to enlist, every group had to employ some sort of qualified military advisor, and they must not wear military uniforms or ranks. A red armband with a crown and the letters 'GR' (standing for Georgius Rex and showing they were in the service of the crown) was all that would be allowed. Looking at

Members of the Volunteer Training Corps could buy dummy rifles to carry on parade or even on guard dutues.

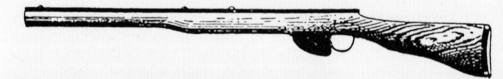

DUMMY RIFLES FOR DRILL   *From* 12/6 *to* 48/-
per dozen.

SHORT LEE-ENFIELD MODEL   CORRECT BALANCE AND WEIGHT
45/- *per dozen.*

Send for Sample and Lists :   SUMMERS, 28, CHEAPSIDE, LONDON.

The Parade Drill Rifle.   AN EXACT COPY OF TH' SHORT LEE - ENFIELD

Correctly Weighted and Balanced. Bolt. Magazine and Trigger, Sights. Slings, Piling Swivel and Adjustable Strap, &c.
As used by Home Defence Leagues for route marching.
10/6 each. Special Prices for Quantities.

On view Central Association Volunteer Training Corps.	Sole Agents: TEPSON & CO., 28, Essex Street, Strand.	Manufacturers: GEMS & GRABHA, Lancaster Road, North Kensington

the retired soldiers and men well over military age who had joined up already, people joked that 'GR' stood for 'God's Rejects' or, the name that would haunt the volunteers for the rest of the war: 'Gorgeous Wrecks'.

Most importantly, they must understand that there would be no government funding: volunteers would have to pay for everything themselves. To become an officer meant taking two courses: the first was a general military syllabus taking up 3 hours per day for six days a week over three weeks, followed by 6 hours of examinations, followed by a drill course lasting 2 hours per day for three weeks costing a total of 3 guineas. Ordinary volunteers had to pay for training in Map Reading, First Aid, Signalling and a host of other skills. When, in 1915, regulations allowed for volunteers to have a special grey/green twill uniform, they had to pay for them. One rule stated that an officer could carry a sword if all his men were armed – but in the West Riding around 12,000 volunteers could muster just 750 rifles between them. A market developed in dummy rifles with wooden models for drill training and metal and wood replicas for guard duties. A major part of volunteer work was simply fund raising.

Wakefield gained its own branch of the Athlete's Volunteer Force by mid September 1914 when up to seventy men per week under the command of Honorary Secretary C. Beaumont attended drill sessions at the Wakefield Trinity ground led by Sergeant Leadbeater with rifle training under Sergeant Major Lingwood at the rifle range in Cradocks Rope Works. In December, a crowded meeting in Council Chambers of the Town Hall and attended by the Bishop of Wakefield, the Chief Constable, Colonel Hind and various other dignitaries, discussed the formation of Wakefield's own official Volunteer Training Corps. The Bishop explained that an invasion was quite possible and the enemy would make straight for industrial areas. 'Unless they had trained men to meet a possible invasion they might as well put women and children to keep soldiers back; they would simply be providing food for the guns.' The Volunteer Training Corps, he explained, would mean that there would at least be some military training available for men who were otherwise unable to serve. 'It was decided to form a corps', the *Yorkshire Post* reported, 'and a large number of men at once joined.'

The Wakefield Volunteer Training Corps was formed in January 1915, organised jointly by Thomas Craven and J.T. Mills, the local

A fund-raising card to support the local VTC. (*Courtesy Kate Taylor*)

agents for the Liberal and Conservative parties, who had abandoned their political differences for the duration of the war. Percy S. Craddock was appointed as the Commandant, and officers from the West Riding Constabulary and Wakefield City Police were brought in as drill instructors. Initially, the Wakefield men were divided into nine companies but this was quickly reduced to just four, with headquarters in the Bull Ring, and communication was largely by means of advertisements placed in the *Wakefield Express* that gave the weekly timetable for route marches, parades and training. Drill parades were held at the new West Riding Police Headquarters in Back Bond Street (now Laburnum Road), at Ings Road School, Wakefield Corn Exchange or at Sandal Council School. Following the December meeting, almost a thousand men from the Wakefield area had signed up from all walks of life, including Wakefield councillors and aldermen, the headmaster and other masters from Queen Elizabeth Grammar School, local solicitors such as W.H. Coles (later Wakefield's diocesan Registrar) and leaders of local industries such as Charles Rhodes of Joseph Rhodes & Sons Ltd, the engineering firm based at Grove Iron Works. Despite the apparent enthusiasm from the Bishop and Chief Constable, an application for a grant from the City Council was refused, so most men paraded in civilian clothes, even after permission to wear the Volunteer uniform was granted.

Cap badge of Wakefield's 10th Battalion.

In terms of war service, though, there was little for the Wakefield Volunteers to do. To begin with 'discipline was almost a matter of choice' until volunteers could be encouraged to sign up to a formal commitment to serve and a system of fines introduced for failures to attend as the initial enthusiasm wore off. Official regulations prevented them from mounting guard unless they had sought permission from the local authorities but as time went on, they were called in to help as sentries at munitions works and to stand guard as prisoners of war were transported through town as well as helping with security at the Lofthouse Camp. For the moment, their activities were limited to alternate weekends when they underwent drill sessions or had a long country walk billed as a more military sounding 'route march'. One Sunday in April 1915, some of them assembled at Newton Lodge, home of company leader and solicitor William H. Kingswell, for a church service, singing 'Fight the good fight' and 'Onward Christian Soldiers' but more often drum-head services were held at Heath Common, attracting a crowd of onlookers. On a Saturday morning in June, the Volunteers met the band of the Yorkshire and Lancashire Regiment at Kirkgate Station and paraded through the streets to the Town Hall in Wood Street and often used their route marches as a means of recruitment, marching on one occasion to Ossett and Horbury and back to Wakefield and on another from Wakefield to Durkar and Crigglestone – where being Wakefield men they knew the best place for a recruitment rally would be the Gardeners Arms.

The unit's secretaries, Craven and Mills, arranged training weekends at country houses including one in August 1915 at Temple Newsam, placed at the Volunteers' disposal by the Hon Edward F.L. Wood, MP. The men marched there from Newton Lodge and were billeted at Colton School, but despite the Saturday outings, many of the men had to be treated for blisters at the end of the journey. The 'Gorgeous Wrecks' name still stuck and the volunteers were often at the receiving end of many jibes, not least from the *Wakefield Express*. During manoeuvres at Heath Common that same month, they practised passing on messages. The paper noted that they played Chinese Whispers and claimed that the information 'The enemy approaching in force' became, as it was repeated, 'The enemy entering on all fours'! The reporter also remarked that 'the slackers slacked and the lukewarm followed the maxim of pleasure as usual.' On another occasion, they carried out 'tactical exercises' at Heath Common when, according to the paper, the swampy nature of the ground 'caused the experience to be the reverse of comfortable.'

By September, when they were inspected on the playing field of the Grammar School, they were beginning to look the part, and a new branch, the Motor Volunteers, had been formed for anyone who owned a vehicle. They soon found themselves busy transporting the wounded and providing lifts for soldiers home on leave as well as training for a role supporting the other volunteers in case of attack. Later that month they marched to Nostell Priory, spending two nights at Wragby School as part of a weekend filled with early morning drill, a Sunday parade at Wragby Church, a route march, and a chance to look round the grounds of the hall. There was good food and an evening smoking concert in the Riding School in the Priory grounds with the Volunteers themselves providing the entertainment. They were awoken on Monday at 6.00am to march back to Wakefield, and the general impression was one of a jolly outing that at least one Wakefield soldier objected to. In a letter to the *Wakefield Express* he, like many others, took the view that the Volunteers were a way of avoiding real service: 'I was reading about their marching to Nostell Priory. I wonder how they would like walking single file down a

An unidentified member of the West Riding Volunteers.

gutter in the road swept by German machine gun fire in order to make our way to the trenches.'

By October most men had some sort of uniform. In November, they were issued with a new cap badge, paid for out of his own pocket by Percy Cradock. As 1915 drew to a close, Kitchener himself acknowledged the useful role the VTC was playing in preparing men for military service. The demand for more troops at the front had brought a reduction in medical standards, and many who had been rejected as totally unfit in 1914 found that a year later they had no difficulty in passing the military medical examination. The coming of conscription in 1916 meant that volunteers of military age were increasingly subject to being called up, and the role of the corps began to change. Military tribunals often required men to join the VTC as a condition of their exemption so that even those who would not be going out to France would have at least some sort of training in case the feared invasion ever did come to pass – still seen as a very real possibility as late as the summer of 1918.

The involvement of a VTC unit in fighting during the Easter Rising in Dublin came at a time when the military had recognised the role of volunteers and finally accepted them as members of the armed forces. Volunteers could now officially call themselves soldiers and the Wakefield Volunteers were now known as 10th Battalion West Riding Volunteers. As soldiers, they were now expected to work even harder, and throughout that summer they were involved in increasingly demanding training with a field day at Methley Park, by permission of Lord Mexborough, in June. There were ambitious manoeuvres at Lindale Hill, Wrenthorpe, in September 1916, when the Volunteers marched through Potovens to encounter an 'enemy' made up of men from the 2nd Battalion Heavy Woollen District Volunteers. It was a good day for the Wakefield men who captured some of their 'spies' and their wagons. A month later they were given training on the railway line close to Stanley Station to learn how to work with trains in the event of an invasion. The Wakefield Motor Squadron was invited to form the nucleus of the 5th Battalion National Motor Volunteers but chose to remain independent, although realising that it would need every car and motorbike in the district to achieve the necessary numbers. By December 1916 it had available 141 cars, 62 lorries, 2 motor ambulances and 69 motor-cycles and sidecars operating from a base in Vicarage Street.

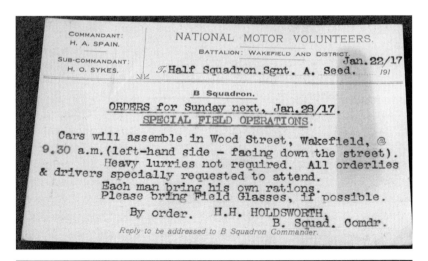

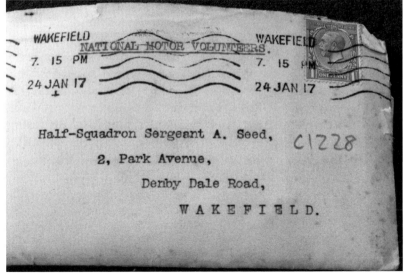

Orders were delivered by post for VTC exercises. (*Courtesy Kate Taylor*)

It was not all work, though. Normally the Corps operated together but individual companies also undertook their own recruiting and social events. In July 1916 'C' company held a sports day at Kettle-thorpe where the grounds of Kettlethorpe Hall were opened for the public, and Crigglestone Band played. There was an inter-platoon tug-of-war and races for children. Although there was no August Bank Holiday, the Volunteers held a gala in early September in

Clarence Park where among the attractions was a demonstration by the newly qualified men from the Wakefield Mines Rescue Station and members of the Voluntary Aid Detachment – the ambulance and nursing organisation – came to give a demonstration of searching for the wounded, bandaging, and carrying stretchers to a dressing station. The Volunteers themselves arranged boxing bouts and a tug-of-war. Other Sports Days in the park were used as fund raisers with the help of Wakefield City Prize Band and Wakefield Old Band who provided the music. A strong sense of camaraderie had developed among the men and when not on duty, the Volunteers also arranged social activities for themselves with a series of smoking concerts at the Strafford Arms in the Bull Ring and the Bull Hotel at the top of Westgate.

By 1917, the Volunteers had become part of the local community and the jokes about 'God's Rejects' had dwindled. Standards of professionalism were rising and the long walks in the countryside had gone. When the Volunteers had a Whitsuntide camp at Nostell Priory in 1917, the Motor Squadron tested their efficiency by making a midnight attack, and battle drills were taken very seriously. By that summer, the Volunteer Corps was fully recognised nationally and its men were provided with uniforms and equipped with rifles and bayonets by the government. Each soldier was required to do 10 hours drill a month and to be able to walk 5 miles carrying equipment as a minimum requirement, and anyone granted exemption if they joined would be called up if they failed to meet their commitment to train.

There was still time for fun. At the 1917 sports event, there was a race planned for girls working on munitions but none of them came forward so instead the runners were all schoolgirls. Elsewhere fourteen of the Volunteer officers vied with each other to demonstrate their martial skills with a competition to decorate a lady's hat and were expected to parade in their creations for the judging. The inability of some to even thread a needle suggested that holding it near the refreshment tent may have been a mistake. As 1918 dawned, the threat of invasion remained and the Volunteers were seen as potentially needed in case the Russian Revolution inspired dissidents in Britain to follow suit. The risk of Irish Republican attacks in the wake of the Dublin Rising was still seen as real and the ever present threat of invasion across the North Sea remained. Whitwood Amateur Dramatic Society performed 'The Duke of Killiecrankie' at Wakefield Empire on 23 February 1918 to raise further funds for the Volunteer Corps. It was well attended.

Another restructuring of the Volunteer Training Corps took place and Wakefield unit became the 1st (Volunteer) Battalion Kings Own Yorkshire Light Infantry. Percy Cradock, now accorded the title of Major, remained the commanding officer of a unit that had grown so much that it now even had its own band. In March 1918, a huge German offensive in France revived fears of an invasion and from all over the country the Volunteers were asked to find 15,000 men to form 'Special Service Companies' for full-time duty on the east coast where they would remain until August, when it was clear the crisis was over. That was when the Wakefield unit went away for its most ambitious camp yet when 26 officers and 336 men travelled by special train from Kirkgate Station for eight days at Withernsea. They were reminded on arrival in no uncertain tones that they were under military orders and this was not just a holiday at the seaside. After a tour of the war defence trenches along the coast they practised 'entrenchment' themselves. They engaged in rifle shooting, bayonet fighting and anti-gas drills as well as fieldcraft and tactics. They had

Trenches on the East Coast of Yorkshire.

route marches of 8 miles or more and a swimming competition at Withernsea baths. On Sunday night the air-raid sirens sounded and they moved from the camp to nearby fields from where they witnessed what was described as a 'splendid display' of anti-aircraft fire, but it was the nearest they would ever come to actual war and the last of their excursions.

Women's work

In September 1914, official figures showed that 190,000 women were officially unemployed nationally. By October, the figure had fallen to 139,000 and by December it stood at around 75,000. But while an estimated 5 million women were in work at the start of the war, almost 13 million were not. Paid labour was still very much a male dominated realm and women were expected to stay at home. Not everyone, of course, was happy with that idea and in common with other towns Wakefield had its own branches of the Suffrage Movement as part of the wider political battle for equal rights. In early July 1913 Florence Beaumont, of Hatfield Hall, organiser of the non-militant Womens Suffrage Society, had helped arrange the reception of a large-scale march of women to London. After passing through Leeds where a rally at Woodhouse Moor had attracted 8,000 people, the march headed south to Wakefield and another rally at the bottom of Kirkgate. Although such demonstrations attracted sympathy, the more militant suffragettes were seen as little more than domestic terrorists with their campaign of arson and bomb attacks on property and even physical assaults. In November 1913, four suffragettes had ambushed the prime minister's car on a trip to Scotland, throwing pepper at him and trying to hit him with a dog whip. On 21 March 1914 the Chancellor of the Exchequer, Lloyd George, was on his way to a meeting in Huddersfield but left the train in Wakefield to avoid a threatened suffragette protest.

Writing to the *Yorkshire Post* in June 1914, C. Ashmore-Ash, of St John's Avenue in Wakefield, claimed that 'the disease of injustice is rife, deep seated and you do not seek to cure the disease but punish the sufferers', and argued that 'women need to be fed equally as well as men but their pay does not admit of it.' The editor's response seemed almost guaranteed to fuel the flames: 'Our correspondent must revise her facts before we can discuss the fancies or assumptions of which her letter chiefly consists. We take one or two "facts". The first has to do with the theory that women are (possibly) inferior

industrial workers because they are underfed, because they are not
paid equally with men, and that equality of pay would lead to
equality of feeding. Among people who have no need to stint it is a
fact that, on the average, it costs less to feed a women than to feed a
man. The larger animal takes the more food. If Miss Ashmore-Ash
inquires she will find that lodging house keepers will board and feed a
woman for less than a man; she will also find – as we have through
careful inquiry – that the cost of feeding young men and women
in such institutions as training colleges is approximately 11s to 9s.
Therefore … she is wrong in her first statement of facts.' War
brought about a truce in the battle of the sexes with the various
branches of the Movement agreeing to suspend their activities in the
national interest, but at the same time it would provide women with
opportunities few could have dreamt of to prove themselves equal
citizens. Almost immediately, committees sprang up dedicated to supporting the soldiers by knitting socks, scarves and other 'comforts' or
by raising money to send parcels to men serving abroad. Others
established groups to provide aid to families of servicemen or to help
the refugees arriving in Britain in their thousands. Isabella O. Ford,

War workers.

of Leeds, for example, set up an office in Room 48 at County Hall, Wakefield for the collection and distribution of clothes to the needy of the area and 'particular consideration will be given to the wants of Belgian refugees.' All these were seen as respectable female occupations, not far removed from the pre-war charity work ladies of leisure had indulged in but, useful as these activities were, women would soon be called upon to do much more.

The outbreak of the war affected all aspects of the economy but especially luxury goods and other services where large numbers of women were employed. Domestic servants were not only employed by the wealthy, many aspiring middle-class families had at least one servant in their home, but as men enlisted and incomes fell, they found themselves out of work. At the same time, export orders for the mills and factories were cancelled and many laid off or put on short time. Within weeks, though, orders began coming in for military uniforms and equipment, and as the men marched away, vacancies began to open up in all kinds of jobs. Women took over running small businesses and took over roles traditionally seen as 'men's work', with journalists referring to 'petrol nymphs' working as van drivers or 'conductorettes' appearing on the trams.

Women with specialist medical skills came forward to volunteer for service in France but were rejected. Dr Elsie Inglis, a trained surgeon and psychiatrist was told by the War Office to 'go home and keep quiet' as the last thing the army needed was hysterical women in the war zone. Private enterprises arranged ambulance units and women volunteered to work alongside the French and Belgian armies, who showed a more accepting attitude but it still took some time before female volunteers reached the British army. Among them was Nellie Spindler, born in September 1891 and the daughter of Police Sergeant George and Elizabeth Spindler, of 104 Stanley Road, Wakefield. In 1911 Nellie was a hospital nurse at the City Fever Hospital on Park Lane, Wakefield and moved to the Township Infirmary in Leeds where she worked from 1912 to 1915. In November 1915 she took up a post at Whittington Military Hospital in Litchfield and worked there until

Nellie Spindler.

the opportunity came up in May 1917 to act as a staff nurse with the Queen Alexandra's Imperial Military Nursing Service, at Abbeville in France. That summer she moved to No. 44 Casualty Clearing Station (CCS), a British evacuation hospital at Brandhoek, in Belgium, that specialised in abdominal wounds. Because those wounds needed urgent treatment the Clearing Station was positioned close to the front and to a railway line that was the target of frequent shelling.

On Tuesday, 21 August 1917, the clearing station came under fire from German artillery. Kate Luard, the sister in charge of 32 CCS, which was alongside 44 CCS at the time of the attack, later wrote: 'I expected [for one rash day] to be telling you all about Tuesday at home tomorrow, but must write it now. The business began about 10.00am. Two [shells] came pretty close after each other and both just cleared us and No. 44. The third crashed between Sister E[lizabeth Eckett]'s ward in our lines and the Sisters' Quarters of No. 44. Bits came over everywhere, pitching at one's feet as we rushed to the scene of the action, and one just missed one of my Night Sisters getting into bed in our Compound. I knew by the crash where it must have gone and found Sister E. as white as paper but smiling happily and comforting the terrified patients. Bits tore through her Ward but hurt no one. Having to be thoroughly jovial to the patients on these occasions helps us considerably ourselves. Then I came on to the shell-hole and the wrecked tents in the Sister's Quarters at 44. A group of stricken [Medical Officers] were standing about and in one tent the Sister was dying. The piece went through her from back to front near her heart. She was only conscious a few minutes and only lived 20 minutes. She was in bed asleep. The Sister who shared her tent had been sent down the day before because she couldn't stand the noise and the day and night conditions. The Sister who should have been in the tent which was nearest was out for a walk or she would have been blown to bits; everything in her tent was; so it was in my empty Ward next to Sister E. It all made one feel sick.' Nellie's friend, Minnie Wood, was also from Wakefield and wrote home to the Spindler family that 'your daughter became unconscious immediately she was hit and she passed away perfectly peacefully just 20 minutes afterwards. I was with her at the time but after the first minute or two she did not know me. It was a great mercy she was oblivious to her surroundings for the shells continued to fall in for the rest of the day.' Both Elizabeth Eckett and Minnie Wood later received the Military Medal for their bravery during the attack. Today Nellie lies as the only woman among the 10,000 men buried in Lijssenthoek Military Cemetery. There are always flowers on her grave.

In 1914, only adventurous young women from reasonably wealthy families could afford to travel out to France and Belgium to do their bit behind the lines, funding their own travel and expenses but often doing remarkable work. The First Aid Nursing Yeomanry, for example, was a distinctly upper-class paramilitary association whose women had to own or be able to hire a horse and who were admitted only on the recommendation of an existing member, but its volunteers drove ambulances and ran canteens across the Western Front, collecting an impressive number of gallantry awards in the process. Others, like Elsie Knocker and her friend Mairie Chisholm, set up and ran a small independent field hospital of their own. Not surprisingly, their adventures made for great propaganda both for the government and, more importantly, for the suffrage movement, but few could afford to follow their example. Plenty of people were needed to assist the Voluntary Aid Detachments in every town but the 'voluntary' part meant that not many working women could find the time to help out on a regular basis and VAD work fell to those who could afford to give their time freely. Those women without family dependants joined the various organisations that grew during the war, working as 'lumberjills' on forestry projects or on farms with the Women's Land Service Corps. Some enlisted in Queen Mary's Auxiliary Army Corps – 'the girl behind the man behind the gun' as their recruiting slogan ran – and went out to France as clerks, drivers and various other duties around the huge base depots established along the French coast.

At home, women were increasingly visible in all kinds of roles but one group was more obvious than others. In the heavy woollen districts, a yellow dye known as picric acid had always been treated with caution because of its explosive qualities but by 1915 it was being used as an ingredient in 'Lyddite', the main type of explosive used in British artillery shells. Those working with it in munitions factories found that although its use might have changed, its ability to stain had not. Over time, skin, hair and eyes absorbed small quantities of picric acid and 'munitionettes', as they were often known, soon acquired another nickname – 'canaries'. Yellow-faced munitions workers were immediately identifiable in the street as they made their way to and from work. Comic though they may have looked, in fact the chemicals were slowly poisoning them. Symptoms associated with working with explosives included nose bleeds, headaches, sore throats, nausea, bowel problems, skin rashes, anorexia, drowsiness and swelling of the hands and feet. A study at the Woolwich Arsenal showed that all workers reported a bitter taste in their mouths, poor appetites and constipation whilst around a quarter of women claimed to suffer skin problems or that their periods were affected with over a third reporting feelings of depression and irritability. Some symptoms probably owed more to food shortages, family stress and long working hours but at least 349 cases of serious TNT poisoning were recorded during the war of whom 109 are known to have died.

In the initial rush to volunteer, industry had lost huge numbers of skilled men, so much so that some had to be brought back to work in uniform at their old jobs but the damage was already done. The army needed to feed its guns but at home, industry was struggling to keep up. The existing munitions factories were not enough to meet demand but the businesses switching to war production were inexperienced, leading to what became known as the 'shell scandal' of early 1915 when a major offensive on the Western Front failed, apparently

Women at work at the Rhodes factory. (*Courtesy of Kate Taylor*)

because there were not enough shells, and so many of those actually fired failed to explode. It was hardly surprising since the skills needed to build complex ammunition took time to develop and most manufacturers were learning on the job.

The scandal led to the creation of the Ministry of Munitions to oversee war production and to manage the recruitment, training and management of war workers, and especially of female staff. As early as November 1914, workers at Vickers had complained about setting up machines for the first women workers, and trade unions were strongly opposed to what they called the 'dilution' of skilled labour, so a series of compromises were reached in March 1915 to allow women and boys to operate semi- or completely automatic machinery, on the grounds that it was not skilled work, but would allow them to do parts of a skilled man's job but leaving the final work to him. Further moves came with the Dilution Scheme in October and the Substitution Scheme the following year, which allowed women to take on increasingly skilled tasks.

The Ministry brought together over ninety leading businessmen to act as advisors and to create local 'Boards' to manage production. On 16 April 1915, Wakefield was among the first areas of the country to organise its resources when a small Munitions Committee was elected at a meeting of manufacturers convened by the Mayor of Wakefield. They immediately set to work to compile an inventory of local machinery and reported that all the firms taking part were engaged either directly or indirectly on War Office work. Ossett firms like J. Halstead & Son, J. Redgwick & Sons and Moses & Naylor all agreed to work together as part of a shell-making scheme. In 1922, the official history of the Ministry of Munitions recorded that the Wakefield Board went on to be unique in being able to produce almost every part of the 18-pdr artillery shell: '... to produce shell forgings', the history recorded, 'a large press designed for the pressing of steel boats and a 1,250-ton wagon-wheel press were adapted until such time as suitable presses could be obtained. This reason, combined with the necessity of disturbing labour as little as possible, decided the committee to promote co-operative work rather than establish a National Shell Factory, and throughout April and May they organised the former type of scheme ... On 28 May, 1915, an offer to provide forgings for, machine and assemble 2,000 18-pdr. shell weekly was accepted in general terms by the Armaments Output Committee with whom the Wakefield Committee had been for some

Shell factory at work.

time in correspondence.' Finally, on 12 June 1915, an agreement was signed between the new Ministry of Munitions and the Wakefield Committee and within a fortnight of signing, the Board reported that the output of forgings had already begun.

This contract did not arrange for the filling of the shells with shrapnel bullets (each shrapnel shell contained over 300 lead balls, making it essentially like a giant shotgun) but was superseded by a new contract signed on 10 September, when this part of the operation was added. The original contract called for an initial weekly delivery of 2,000 shells, rising to 5,000 as soon as possible but the lack of specialist gauges held up progress in setting up the machinery and the first deliveries could not be made until the beginning of October. Once begun, output steadily increased and the promised 5,000 per week were being sent out by the end of 1915 and by the time of the Armistice Wakefield produced 17,016 shells in a single week.

The Wakefield Board consisted of a Co-operative Group of fifteen firms scattered over a wide district. Two contractors made the shell case forgings with the machining and filling operations (where the explosives and shrapnel were added) distributed among the other manufacturers. Finally, the completed shells were collected at two centres where government inspectors checked the supplies. Unlike most other areas, the Wakefield Board took complete responsibility for every stage of manufacture as direct contractors to the Ministry of Munitions and acted as a single Board of Directors on behalf of the whole group. It was a spectacularly successful scheme, with only two lots of 500 shells each being rejected out of a total output of 1,184,100. A failure rate of .041 per cent was regarded by the Ministry as a stunning success.

Signing the government contracts meant a massive expansion for the firms involved, and women were needed to take on jobs that would normally have gone to men, and as time went on, trained for skilled work despite the best efforts of trade unions to protect their members. The bigger firms even had to build hostels to accommodate workers brought in to keep production running 24 hours per day. In Leeds, the vast Barnbow factory had its own herd of cows to supply its canteen, and some sixty-four trains a day arrived there to move staff to and from work. Women were promised £1 as minimum wage for a 48-hour week (rising to 24s later in the war) but rates varied. Skilled women tool setters at the Woolwich Arsenal could earn £6-6s a week and £5 per week for female workers was not unusual. A special 'leavers certificate' prevented a worker finding work in another munitions factory for six weeks after leaving their post to prevent staff moving to higher-paid jobs. By contrast, women working in other areas of war work still had to contend with low wages. Complaints from a Belfast cotton mill claimed that women were paid just 10s-6d for a 55-hour week whilst those working on hand grenade production lines could earn as little as 2½d per hour. Sylvia Pankhurst reported a case of a woman earning just 1s-8d for inserting 400 eyelet holes in canvas used for making kitbags for soldiers, giving her an income of 5s 7d for a 47-hour week.

Despite the huge variations in earning potential, nationally the average wage for women rose from 13s 6d a week in 1914 to around 30–35s by the end of the war. Although rising prices ate into the increases, many women found that they had a disposable income for the first time. Respectable women began to socialise outside the home for the first time and the papers were full of the concerns of moral campaigners worried by the sight of women drinking in pubs without men to buy them their drinks – which in any case would have been illegal under wartime drinking laws. Make up and beauty products became increasingly within the price of ordinary women during 1915, at a time when shortages of material meant that hemlines rose and sleeves shortened. As more leg and underarm became visible, Gillette razors for women appeared on the market in 1915, as did Maybelline make-up, with powder, kohl eyeliner and mascara all becoming popular best sellers. Helena Rubenstein reported an upsurge in demand for face creams from wealthier women volunteering as nurses on the front. Another unexpected outcome of women's war work was the popularisation of knickers as a standard item of clothing. The Queen Mary's Auxiliary Army Corps offered its recruits a uniform but not underwear until it became apparent that working-class women often had none and voluminous bloomers stretching from knees to somewhere around the armpit became standard issue. Elsewhere, munitionettes were required to change out of street clothes and into work overalls before each shift so underwear became more important than in the past.

Worried by the moral risks to young women exposed to the young men in uniform (and vice versa in garrison towns), moral watchdogs claimed that the pre-war annual Territorial camps had always left behind mementos of their long summer evenings in the form of a trail of illegitimate births the following spring. Women Police Patrols were set up to scour parks, back streets, theatres and pubs in order to save young people from themselves. Passing any form of sexually transmitted disease to a serviceman was regarded as a criminal offence calculated to 'aid the enemy', although passing on a disease picked up in a French brothel to a girlfriend whilst on leave wasn't. There were also calls for specialist women social workers to be formed into a department to deal with the flood of unmarried mothers that was expected to materialise at any time. Men who could be traced but who were overseas, it was suggested, could marry by post. 'For those cases where the father, if known, is married already,' one writer suggested, 'if the child is healthy and free from hereditary taint, some sad and bereaved mother, herself left childless, should adopt it, either when the mother has nursed it for a few months; or, if the mother cannot nurse, it could be given at once to the foster mother. Sometimes single women long for a child of their own.' Exactly why a single mother should be forced to give up her child to another single mother was not made clear. In the event, illegitimacy levels during the war actually fell from the rates recorded in 1911.

The war brought many changes for women and their contribution led to changes in the political system and eventually to the power to vote that the Suffrage Movement had fought for. But it came at a cost. Writing in 1916, Monica Cosens described how, for munitionettes, 'it is not only her health she is risking, but her youth as well. As Gran'pa [the skilled supervisor at Cosens' factory] once said: "it makes me sad to see the young girls here; they come in fresh and rosy cheeked, and before a month has passed they are pale and careworn." Gran'pa is right. There is no doubt that the girls become shadow eyed and pale, and the effect of working through the night under the glare of electricity adds many wrinkles beneath their eyes, ageing them beyond their years'. Elsewhere, A.K. Foxwell described the lady principal overlooker at Woolwich Arsenal, who explained to prospective staff that rumours of the cemetery behind the works where explosion victims were buried were untrue. 'We don't have these excitements here ... However, this is war work so don't expect to get a leisurely job. Aren't you willing to do your bit, like the soldiers in the trenches? We mustn't expect *our* work to be easy.'

Children

In October 1914, the West Riding Education Committee at Wakefield heard that no fewer than eight schools in Doncaster had been taken over as billets for troops, affecting around 5000 pupils. Only by careful use of the half-time system under which children split their day between working a shift at a local factory or mill and attending school could the disruption be kept to a minimum. Any Wakefield children hoping for their own schools to be commandeered were disappointed. Men of the local Royal Army Medical Corps had lodged at St Mary's school for a while and Clarendon Road school became a collection point for socks, scarves and other comforts for men going overseas and for clothing to help poor families and refugees but generally school life for most continued as normal. In August, the Provision of Meals (Education) Act was brought in and a Canteen Committee appointed to make sure that all local children would get at least one meal a day. A study by the local Medical Officer had shown that Wakefield children started school physically bigger than the national average but left less healthy than most. The fact that so many were from poor families and worked in demanding jobs for half the day before coming to school was not considered to be a factor.

Wakefield Grammar School soon addressed issues around the war. On 25 September the school debating society discussed the motion that 'In the opinion of this House, warfare is necessary to civilisation, and that which it attains cannot be otherwise achieved.' Various speakers took part but despite the tales of German atrocities that

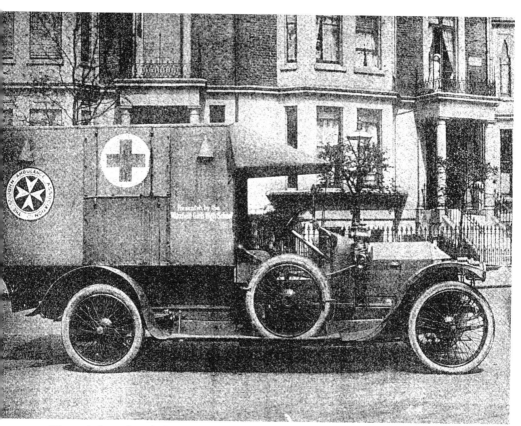

The ambulance bought by the pupils of Wakefield Girls High School.

filled the newspapers, the motion lost 14–7. A few months later, after the famous Christmas Truce of 1914, another debate 'That Germans and Allies singing carols together is incompatible with Germans and Allies trying to annihilate each other.' It, too, lost, this time by 7–1. It was soon followed by 'German nature has gone back, *i.e.* is a throw back to the nature of savages.' The motion was lost by 9–4. Whatever else, the students of Wakefield Grammar did not blindly accept anti-German propaganda. A list was placed in the School Hall of Old Boys who had enlisted into the forces but the school magazine noted that 'other names are known to the School authorities, of those who have offered themselves but have been rejected on physical grounds: to these we offer our special sympathy.' Those serving covered the whole spectrum of ranks with J.W. Stead listed as Colonel, commanding the City of Leeds Battalion (Leeds Pals) with half a dozen fellow old boys serving as privates under him. By mid 1915, 255 names were on the list. Realising that Grammar School boys would be regarded as prime candidates for promotion, Company Drill using dummy rifles was quickly introduced and, with the Headmaster

Scouts assist in the harvest.

acting as Company Commander, six squads had progressed on to training on a rifle range.

Council schools were not in a position to offer weapons training, but 'Swedish Drill' had been part of the syllabus for the past ten years, partly as a cheap form of exercise for schools who couldn't afford sports equipment but also as a way of instilling discipline into children who had often been left to fend for themselves in the poorer areas of town. At the turn of the century the West Riding Education Committee had limited physical education to just 30 minutes per week but by 1913 its teacher-training college at Bingley included drill, organised games and 'rhythmic movement' as part of its course. By then it had also employed military trainers to teach children how to march and even set up drill competitions. Other areas had even brought in dummy rifles for nursery-age children to train with.

The war was brought into the classroom where maps showed the Western Front with the progress of battles marked and updated regularly but more practically, children were put to work knitting for the troops or sewing mailbags and sandbags. Schools enthusiastically raised money and encouraged children to help collect on flag days for a wide variety of causes. Later in the war, the Education Committee was an active part of a campaign to have children collect sphagnum moss for use as packing for medical dressings and to collect chestnuts. These, allegedly, could be processed to create acetone for use in explosives but in reality they were not very effective and thousands of tons collected across the country were eventually left rotting at collecting depots.

School staff dwindled as male teachers went away to war and class sizes grew but their efforts went unappreciated. In 1916, Councillor Mellor provoked a furious reaction when he claimed that 'almost every class was suffering from the war with the exception of teachers' and that they should think about labourers working 54 hours a week. By then, staff shortages meant classes at some schools had reached fifty or even sixty pupils and in extreme cases, teachers were trying to teach two classes at once with the aid of 'pupil apprentices' acting as assistants. As an angry group of Wakefield teachers pointed out in a letter to the *Yorkshire Post*, a female teacher could earn a lot more in other jobs than the 17s 4d per week on offer to them. 'They would find employment of a much less exacting intellectual nature, and certainly more remunerative, on the rear platform of a Wakefield tramcar. War bonuses have been granted by the government to their postal employees, to the railway employees, the munition and other workers; all these are not labourers. The teachers of Wakefield, however, did not ask for a war bonus.' By 1917, they not only asked for a bonus, they demanded it at a meeting of 500 local teachers at the Cathedral Boys School. It emerged that some had been offered an extra 2s 10d per week, others 1s 11d whilst many more had been offered nothing. The teachers declined the offer and instead held out for the 11 per cent bonus Councillor Mellor's colleagues had awarded to Corporation officials.

It was outside school that children played their most active part in the war. In 1908, Baden-Powell had launched the Boy Scout movement with the aim of encouraging boys to learn skills that would allow them to serve their country. The outbreak of war was the first test of how successful his plans had been and as early as 11 August, the Boy Scout uniform was officially recognised 'as that of a public service', and wearing of it by anyone not a member of a recognised troop was made a criminal offence. A sense of how important scouts had very quickly become comes from an advert in the *Middlesex Chronicle* that all 'soldiers, sailors, territorials, scouts, nurses and all persons in uniform' would be photographed for free at a local photographer's studio. In September 1914 volunteers of the 1st and

4th Wakefield Scouts, under Scoutmaster Cecil Robinson, left for a month's tour of duty, living in tents at the Coastguard station at Newton-on-Sea in Northumberland. There they began working as coast watchers on 2-hour shifts day and night to provide warning of any enemy ships crossing the North Sea. By mid October, after they volunteered for a second month's duty, a cottage had been found to house the patrol and by November a five-room cottage, now named 'The Hydro' was home to the boys during their spare time. It was a rugged stretch of coast but despite being out at night in all weather, Scoutmaster Robinson assured families at home that the boys were 'in excellent health'.

Scoutmaster Robinson would soon take on a new role in London when a new 'Scout Defence Force' was formed with the idea that Scouts aged 15 to 17 should be trained as infantrymen for home defence. 'In case of invasion,' explained Chief Scout Baden-Powell, 'a boy of 16 trained to discipline and marksmanship would be worth a dozen men trained to nothing in particular.' In May 1915 it was noted that Birmingham had 600 boys who had been awarded the newly created 'Red Feather' badge of the trained rifleman and that Leicester had 250 but there were none at all in the whole of Yorkshire. It was with a great deal of pride that Cecil Robinson returned to Wakefield in his new role as Staff Officer of the Scout Defence Force, on Saturday, 18 September, to inspect the first unit in Yorkshire to pass the requirements to be accepted. Fifty local scouts paraded of whom thirty had passed their rifle proficiency test by placing seven shots in a 4-inch circle at 25 yards. They became the first in Yorkshire to gain the Red Feather and other War Service badges were awarded to those who had served as coast guards or in other roles with the district efficiency cup going to the 5th Wakefield (Zion) Troop.

The following month around 230 Wakefield scouts paraded for their annual church service conducted that year by Scoutmaster A.L. Leeper and attended by the Bishop of Wakefield. The Bishop spoke of the 2,000 scouts who had enlisted and some of whom had already died as well as the 1,500 scouts still active as coast watchers. 'This was a time,' he told them, 'when everybody able ought to do something, and so far as the Scouts were concerned he would say to them that if they were going to be great they would have to be honourable and pure hearted, have minds not lifted up to vanity and silliness and be kindly towards their neighbours.' Scouts had thrown themselves into war work with gusto, volunteering to guard water supplies against the threat of German agents, acting as messengers for the army and the emergency services, helping with harvesting, assisting the settlement of refugees and working to help at convalescent hospitals for the wounded. In August 1916 1st Wakefield (City) Troop were hard at work on yet another project organised by Lady Catherine Milnes Gaskell, this time to pick fruit and make jam for wounded soldiers in hospitals in Wakefield and Bradford, and each summer groups of scouts and guides went away to work camps to help harvest essential crops. Prime Minister David Lloyd George was quoted in a special edition of *The Times History of the War*, describing the role scouts and guides played in helping Britain win the war: 'It is no small matter to be proud of the fact that the Association was able within a month of the outbreak of war to give the most energetic and intelligent help in all kinds of service. When the boyhood of a nation can give such practical proofs of its honour, straightness and loyalty there is not much danger of that nation going under, for these boys are in training to render service to their country as leaders in all walks of life in the future.'

As with every generation, elders complained about the behaviour of the young and assumed that the lack of fatherly discipline would lead to chaos on the streets. In November 1916 Wakefield's School Attendance Officer said that the attendance of children at school was 'shocking' and blamed 'indifference on the part of the mother.' The State Children's Society wrote an open letter to the *Yorkshire Post* in 1916 that 'an outcry has been raised against what is termed the growing depravity of children, and severer and more repressive punishments are demanded.' The Society explained that the shortage of police, streets darkened by the blackout and the 'exciting influences of sensational cinema shows', as well as what were seen as lenient sentences passed by the courts, had all been blamed for what many saw as a growing juvenile crime wave but pleaded for a system that didn't just lock children away for years on end. Using language that would still be current a century later, one faction argued for ever more harsh penalties whilst another argued that punishment was not enough to break the complex cycle of problems facing some young people. Then, as now, the criminal few attracted all the attention.

Throughout the war children suffered. When food shortages became severe, school attendances fell because small children were needed to stand in food queues to mark the place for their harassed mothers – one in one queue, another in the next, standing for hours in the cold and wet to help keep their families fed. They collected moss, chestnuts, acorns and animal fodder and stood on streets with collection boxes. They ran errands for wounded soldiers or volunteered to put on shows to entertain them. Some committed crimes, most didn't. Most of all though, they waited for news of their fathers and brothers.

Hospitals

It was only in 1908 that it was realised that in case of invasion, there were no hospitals set aside for treating wounded part-time soldiers of the Territorial Force as there were for the Regular army. Across the Empire there were only around 300 trained military nurses and none at all for the Territorials, so the reforms of the army created a new Territorial Force Nursing Service (TFNS) along with a Queen Alexandra's Imperial Military Nursing Service Reserve for those who had served as military nurses but returned to civilian life. Plans were drawn up for the creation of twenty-three territorial force hospitals in towns and cities throughout the country, each with planned accommodation for 520 patients and a staff of ninety-one trained nurses. To qualify for appointment as a sister or staff nurse in the TFNS, candidates had to be over 23 years of age and must have completed three years training in a recognised hospital or infirmary.

The problem was that there was a chronic shortage of fully-trained nurses in the country and some members of the Army Nursing Board were against any sort of military nursing service that recruited from the staff of civilian hospitals in peacetime. Sydney Holland, later Lord Knutsford, and Chairman of the London Hospital, was always opposed to the idea of a military nursing reserve because he felt that if the need arose there would be no difficulty in finding nurses for the army, but to allow women to enrol as individuals in a military reserve could leave civilian hospitals in the difficult position in wartime of losing their most experienced staff to military service. As a result, there was no encouragement and little reward for those who offered their services. Volunteers willing to act as matrons in the TFNS were to spend just seven days training in a military hospital every second year, but nurses who joined would get neither pay nor special training during peacetime in return for their commitment. They were required to declare their intention to serve on 1 January of each year while continuing to work in civilian hospitals where it was

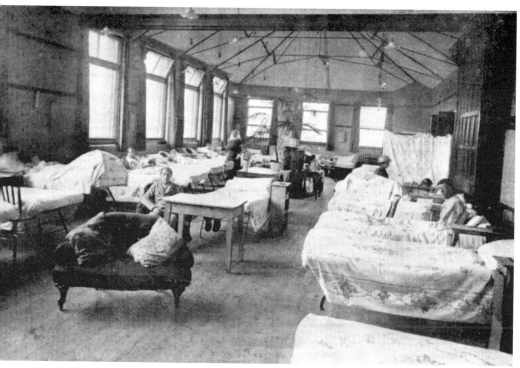

A Voluntary Aid Detachment ward in Clayton Hospital. (*Courtesy Kate Taylor.*)

felt that day to day nursing would provide ample training for whatever might happen in wartime. The only recognition for their offer would be a silver service badge, the design based on the 'double A' cipher of Queen Alexandra, which was to be worn on the right side of their dress or apron during the normal course of their civilian duty – if they were given special permission by their employer to wear it.

The plans for large Territorial Force hospitals were hampered somewhat by the fact that they would not come into existence until war was declared. Buildings were identified but there was no budget for equipment or storage. Everything would have to be found once the go-ahead was given. It is a testament to the organizational skills of those involved that by the end of August 1914, nineteen hospitals were up and running, with the remaining four following close behind in September. In the first week of the war, Leeds' new Teacher Training College at Beckett Park was handed over by Leeds City Council to become the 2nd Northern General Hospital that would be staffed by over 2,000 and included a 126-bed unit for limbless men from Yorkshire, Lincolnshire, Nottinghamshire and Rutland. To the south, 3rd Northern General was established in Sheffield with a staff of around 1,400. Around these large hospitals there was to be a network of 'auxiliary' hospitals operating as an annexe to the General

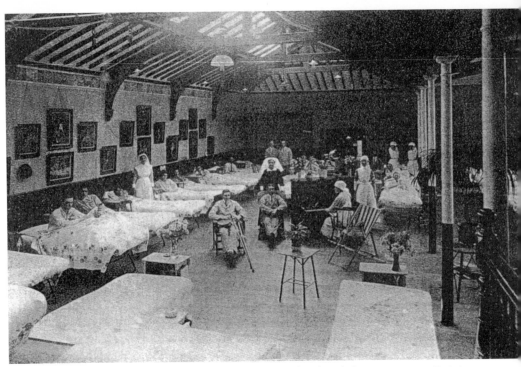

Wakefield was home to several improvised wartime hospitals. (*Courtesy Kate Taylor*)

Hospital, often as 'convalescent' units where men recovering from treatment could be kept under some sort of military control. Often set up in public buildings or even stately homes, these small hospitals were operated by Voluntary Aid Detachments.

Clayton Hospital in Wakefield was quickly earmarked as an auxiliary to Beckett Park and by the end of the first week of war the House Committee agreed that members of St John's Ambulance could work at the hospital to gain practical experience in preparation for voluntary service. Matron was to be asked to provide a list of necessaries to be ordered for the provision of twenty beds for wounded or convalescent soldiers in the Lower Gaskell Ward. Soon after, it was also agreed that voluntary nurses would act as ward maids and waitresses and funding was based on a calculation that each patient cost 1s a day for food and about the same per day for drugs. By the time it opened in November 1914, Clayton Hospital's plans had extended to fifty beds spread between two large wards, named Gaskell and Milnes after their benefactors and three smaller wards under the control of Nellie King as commandant. The first men were brought down from Beckett Park in the private cars of ten Wakefield citizens, including that of Lady Catherine Milnes Gaskell, and there was an immediate appeal launched for gifts with an emphasis on cigarettes, pipes and tobacco. The hospital also asked for counterpanes and bedlinen as well as pyjamas and other necessities.

Lady Catherine Milnes Gaskell was determined to see the men well provided for. Each patient was initially allotted a budget of just 2s a week for food by the War Office, so she wrote to Lady St Oswald at Nostell Priory to ask whether her ladyship could spare any rabbits so that she could make pies for them. Lord St Oswald responded immediately by sending an initial ten pairs. In April 1915 she was in action again, this time with an appeal for croquet sets, one for Clayton VAD hospital and one for Thornes House where she planned to entertain wounded soldiers on two days a week for fishing and to play croquet in her grounds. At Christmas, the King himself provided a hamper for the patients, some of whom were fit enough to be discharged or at least able to go home for the holiday so that only eight patients remained in the hospital. They were invited to hang up stockings which were filled – or indeed over-filled – by Mrs Welch, the wife of the Vicar of Wakefield. On Boxing Day they had a visit from Lady Allendale of Bretton Hall and her daughters, who put on an entertainment consisting of dramatic sketches, songs and pianoforte solos.

The aim of the network of auxiliary hospitals was to enable men to be treated as near to home and family as possible but it did not always work. In May 1916, Frederick Baldwin of the Hampshire Regiment, who had been 'shockingly wounded' at Ypres, died exactly a year after being admitted. He had no known relatives or friends but had been a pleasant and uncomplaining patient who had become something of a favourite with the staff. Commandant Nellie King made arrangements for his funeral in Wakefield Cemetery where his coffin was carried by members of the Voluntary Aid Detachment. All patients who were able to attended, along with fifty officers and men of the guard from Lofthouse Park internment camp, who provided a firing party salute at the graveside. Nursing staff, kitchen staff, the patients and many private individuals laid wreaths and flowers in front of a large crowd of local people.

Alongside Clayton Hospital's contribution, in August 1914 Walton Church Committee offered their new Sunday school building to the St John Ambulance Brigade as a convalescent hospital soon after war broke out, but at the time the Brigade was busy with plans to convert the newly-built police headquarters into a 100-bed unit. The plans were quietly shelved in September, but as casualties increased, Clayton Hospital became too small and in any case the wards were

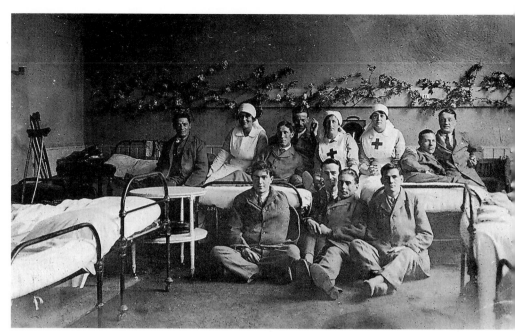

VAD nurses and some of their charges, 1917.

needed for local civilian patients. At the end of July 1916, Clayton's Minute Books reported: '30.7.1916 Cannot provide more beds for soldiers – needs of other patients and kitchen could not cope'. By March 1917 the Mayor of Wakefield, Councillor Edmund Stonehouse, was under pressure from the government to find alternative and larger accommodation.

That month two representatives of Northern Command, Colonel Dunscombe and Colonel Littlewoood, inspected the Georgian mansion at Wentworth House in Wentworth Street and declared it 'excellently suited' for a hospital with only minor alterations to create two more lavatories. It had been the home of Wakefield Girls High School since its foundation in 1878 and had over 400 pupils in seventeen forms occupying a total of thirty-eight rooms. At a special meeting with Stonehouse, the governors agreed to hand the building over for use as an auxiliary hospital, and in return Wakefield's Technical College would find rooms for many of the classes. A public meeting followed in April when Stonehouse broke the news that the War Department would provide nothing more than the standard rate which had risen to 3s per patient per day. Wakefield people and the local branch of the Red Cross would therefore need to find £1,000 to equip the building and £2,000 a year to run it. The headmistress of the High School, Gertrude McCroben, was given no say in the decision but found herself landed with the task of organising everything instead of taking a break over Easter. In early April, pupils of the High School and Grammar School removed all the desks and other school items, leaving only a piano. From then on, until the summer of 1919, the girls were taught at 8 St John's North, 4 St John's Square, rooms at Wakefield Technical College, or in marquees erected on the school playing field in Blenheim Road. A room in the Cathedral vicarage, then in Sandy Walk, became the school office.

Commandant King took charge of Wentworth House, now known as St John's Auxiliary Hospital when it was formally opened on 8 May 1917 and the nursing staff were, again, those who had trained under the VAD. Dr J.W. Walker, better remembered today as the author of *A History of Wakefield*, offered his services as the hospital's Medical Officer. Mrs King seems to have been efficient, but not necessarily popular. When another military hospital, known as Park Lane Auxiliary Hospital, was established in a part of the Wakefield Union Workhouse in Park Lodge Lane, the Board of Guardians, who had responsibility for the Workhouse, were keen to assure locals that there would be no additional call on the rates. But although the Guardians had decided at the outbreak of war that they could accommodate some wounded soldiers, for some reason they refused to give Mrs King charge of them.

Already under pressure to treat a growing number of wounded soldiers, the managers of Clayton Hospital were asked in November 1917 to provide medical care for the Conscientious Objectors housed in Wakefield Work Centre, but agreed they would not do so. A month later, an approach was made to Clayton Hospital by Dr Littlewood, from Leeds, for Northern Command to discuss medical care for interned civilian prisoners from Lofthouse Park Camp. The suggestion was that where necessary prisoners could be admitted to Clayton as in-patients. The offer was that the hospital would receive 5s a day to cover their care but no guard would be provided, and the Hospital would be responsible if any of their prisoner patients staged a miraculous recovery and escaped. Perhaps not surprisingly, the Hospital committee minutes simply record, 'Request declined'.

Then, in January 1918, Wakefield's mayor was asked if the city could provide another hospital, this time for convalescent soldiers who would be transferred from the Heavy Woollen District Military Hospital housed in a former workhouse infirmary at Staincliffe, Dewsbury. There was considerable reluctance to ask for yet more support from Wakefield people, but the indefatigable Lady Catherine Milnes Gaskell seems to have been determined that the city could cope, immediately obtaining promises of £2,000 from prominent local citizens. Colonel Smythe offered Heath Hall at a nominal rent and workmen moved there in April 1918 to convert the elegant mansion into the White Rose Military Hospital, with beds for 100 soldiers. Appeals again went out for furniture, bed linen, dressing gowns and pyjamas, whilst students at Wakefield and Dewsbury technical colleges made bedside lockers.

Throughout the war, the War Department allowance for the care of the wounded, at 3s a day, was only enough for only a very basic diet, especially when prices continued to rise. Individual Wakefield people, local organisations and schools regularly supplied additions – bacon, sausages, ham, brawn, cakes and fresh fruit, as well as flowers, newspapers and magazines. A group of people led by Mrs Thornhill Simpson, of Walton, began a regular collection of spare eggs, usually over 1,000 a week, from local poultry keepers to keep the local hospitals supplied throughout the war and beyond, with even enough to spare to send to other military hospitals. More appeals brought in playing cards, a gramophone and gramophone records and frequent donations of packets of cigarettes.

Wakefield people, and particularly local schoolchildren, organised concerts to entertain the patients. At Christmas 1917, one of the wards at Park Lane Hospital was converted into a theatre, with scenery provided by the proprietors of Wakefield Theatre Royal and Opera House. Patients and nurses put on a musical play written by one of the men, Sapper Tusker of the Royal Engineers, and somehow each man in a Wakefield hospital was provided with a Christmas stocking. At other times, occupational therapy for the wounded came in the form of making rag rugs. In November 1917 Lady Catherine was again out calling for materials for them such as unwanted flannelette.

Where they were able to walk, they had the freedom of local cinemas. One or two car owners, notably Major Howard Hall of South Parade, and Miss Tew, a leading member of the VAD from Heath, took men out for drives. Just occasionally there was the chance of a mass outing such as the time fifty patients were taken to Charles Roberts' wagon works at Horbury, where they were shown round

Patients of the Wakefield Asylum.

Wakefield Asylum Staff, 1917.

and given a substantial tea. Another, perhaps more attractive excursion was provided by the Yorkshire Tramway Company who took men from Park Lane Hospital to Roundhay Park.

Sheffield, too, was making arrangements for the creation of auxiliary hospitals and one building taken over was the former West Riding Pauper Lunatic Asylum at Wadsley Bridge. In order to turn it into the Wharncliffe Military Hospital, nearly 1,700 inmates had to be relocated to other institutions, at Menston, Storthes Hall and to Stanley Royd Asylum in Wakefield where, by December, there were some 1,260 male and 870 female patients, many, but by no means all, funded by the Board of Guardians. Some were mentally ill but fifteen were simply classified as 'vagrants'. The numbers of patients remained stable over the coming year but the introduction of conscription raised questions about the level of care being provided. In 1916, questions were raised in Parliament concerning the safety of female staff who were increasingly having to cover for their male colleagues who had been called up along with calls for a halt to the conscription of male attendants until asylum authorities were able to replace them with other men. The Home Office Under-Secretary replied that there were female nurses in four of the twenty-four male wards but that they were employed to manage 'quiet cases which can be properly attended by women, boys, sick cases or chronic cases of a quiet class.'

To these were being added a new type of patient. It was not until April 1917 that the Asylums Board received notification from the War Office of a new policy towards 'soldiers and sailors who have become insane during the war.' Until then, any man suffering 'shell-shock' or any other mental condition triggered during his service was treated as a 'pauper' unless he had been awarded a disability pension. From then on, though, servicemen were to be treated as private patients with a budget of 3s 6d per week for their upkeep and 2s 6d extra for 'special comforts'. A suggestion that special suits, like the 'hospital blues' worn by physically wounded soldiers, should be provided was rejected, the Asylums Board refusing to pay 15s 6d and arguing that the military authorities should be responsible for providing the cloth free. The same meeting went on to award the Board a war bonus of 2s per week.

Typical of the type of patient now coming to Wakefield was 28-year-old Beech Jennings from Pontefract and formerly a private in the King's Own Yorkshire Light Infantry. Discharged on 1 July 1918, he was admitted to an asylum in Glamorgan a few days later. His notes record: 'Patient is excited, very loquacious & noisy, incoherent & rambling, exalted & defectively orientated. Does not realise his position, is untidy & unable to look after himself. He shouts loudly & has exaggerated movements in all joints, stares in hostile manner at everyone, is impulsive, emotional & extravagant in ideas. He is a native of Yorkshire, father alive, mother dead, 2 brothers & 2 sisters are alive, 2 brothers were killed in the war, has 2 children. He joined the Army in 1914 & was 2 years in France, has been in Whitchurch.' The record goes on to note that he was 'transferred to York W Riding Asylum, Wakefield – 13 Nov 1918'.

Demand for hospital beds increased during the winter of 1917–18 to the point where marquees had to be erected at both Wentworth House and Park Lodge Lane to take additional patients, and by May 1918 Wentworth House had 256 patients and Park Lane had 147. Gaskell Ward at Clayton Hospital was taken over again to hold servicemen who had been discharged but still needed medical attention before returning to civilian life and consideration was already being given to the long-term needs of rehabilitation. Local company G.E. Appleyard undertook to furnish two wards which were to be set aside for a period of three years to accommodate discharged soldiers

and bought in special massage and electrical equipment for physio-
therapy at a cost of £20.

In December 1918, Mrs Longley, of Thornes Lane, sent £50 to part
endow a bed in memory of her son, Sergeant George William Jubb,
formerly of the Yorkshire Dragoons, who had been killed on 5 September while serving with the new Royal Air Force. In April 1919,
Nellie King wrote to offer £500 from monies left over and told them
that the VAD wanted to endow a bed. The committee noted that
£500 was 'about right'. Whatever the committee and the Board of
Guardians thought of her, Commandant Nellie King went on to be
honoured with the Royal Red Cross Medal and was invested at
Windsor Castle, afterwards going with other recipients of civilian
medals to have tea with Queen Alexandra at Marlborough House.
Miss Percy Tew, the VAD who arranged outings was awarded the
Royal Red Cross Medal (2nd Class) as were her colleagues Miss
Pilkington and Miss Walker. Captain Walker, the medical officer,
was awarded an OBE for his services. From almost nothing, between
them they had created a hospital with a fully equipped operating
theatre where 230 major operations had been performed. In all, 3,131
in-patients and 297 out-patients had passed through Wakefield's
auxiliary hospitals and almost all had been treated by staff who gave
their time freely. In the summer of 1919 the high school girls were
able to return to Wentworth House. Heath Hall stood empty until it
was used as a military hospital again in the second world war. At
Clayton Hospital a roll of honour was started to commemorate
nurses who had been on war service and the idea evolved into a more
lasting memorial in the form of a new nurses home.

CHAPTER 7

Law and DORA

At 7.00pm on the evening of Thursday, 30 July 1914, 26-year-old Tom Harris left home for a ride on his treasured 4hp motorcycle, telling his father he planned to go up to Leeds to pick up some tools. An enthusiastic and experienced rider, Tom had only owned his own bike for six months and was on his way home when he collided with a dray on Lower Road at Oulton. He was taken to hospital with compound fractures of his arm and leg and injuries to his face. He never regained consciousness and died 2 hours later of a fractured skull. An inquest was opened the following day and adjourned until Tuesday, 11 August. His grief stricken father 'expressed his thanks for the uniform courtesy and kindness the police and everyone associated with the case had shown.' As Chief Constable of Wakefield, Tom's father, Thomas Middleton Harris, barely had time to begin to grieve for his son before being overwhelmed by the massive task of maintaining a sense of order when war broke out just days later.

In 1914, the City of Wakefield police were responsible for patrolling the city itself, with the West Riding Constabulary covering the outlying areas and the Grand Central Railway Police operating out of Wakefield Westgate railway station holding responsibility for any offences linked to the railways. All three forces regularly employed ex-servicemen, and within days of the outbreak of war forty-three reservists had been recalled, leaving their stations undermanned. Among them was William Hall, a Wakefield policeman for three years before being ordered back to rejoin 1st Battalion of the Scots Guards, who would be among the city's first casualties when he was killed on 14 September, leaving a widow and two young children. Hall was just one of sixty-three West Riding policemen who would never return.

As the recruiting drives went on, the county's Chief Constable found many of his men, many of them experienced ex-soldiers whose reserve commitment had ended, were increasingly determined to swap

Wakefield City Police.

police blue for army khaki. He finally gave in to pressure and gave his consent for 318 serving officers to volunteer for the military. James Crease of Sandal had served seven years with the Grenadier Guards and had spent nearly three years deployed in the South African War. After leaving the forces he joined the Railway Police and his commitment to the reserve had ended by the time war broke out. In 1915 at the age of 36 he volunteered for the army and enlisted into the Military Foot Police where he was posted to a Traffic Control Company, responsible for keeping the flow of supply trucks to and from the front moving. The job involved him cycling from post to post and a report in the *Wakefield Express* suggested that this contributed to the hernia that caused him to be admitted to hospital in August 1918. As he waited for treatment he was visited in hospital by an old friend from Wakefield, Sergeant J. Ernest Harris (son of Chief Constable Harris and brother of Tom), who reported finding him comfortable and well cared for. Unfortunately, the operation for a strangulated hernia went wrong and he died of peritonitis on 10 August. According to a newspaper report, 'Mrs Crease has been the recipient of very kind and sympathetic letters from Sergeant Harris, Captain Davison, Lance Corporal Beresward, Lieutenant Eastman, the Sister in Charge of the hospital and the Church of England Chaplain. In the course of his letter Captain Davison said Crease "was the finest and most reliable Sergeant it has ever been my good fortune to have met. He was held in high esteem by all the officers and men". Writers of other letters stated that "he was an excellent soldier, who by his devotion to duty and good fellowship won the confidence of the officers and all Company" and "he was a man of fine character, and a true and noble Englishman"'.

With reservists leaving to rejoin their regiments and other officers keen to enlist, chief constables were forced to expand the use of volunteers and the Special Constable's Act of 1914 was hurriedly passed at the end of August. Back in 1820, a law had come into force that allowed magistrates to order citizens to become Special Constables in time of public disorder. Another act in 1831 created a new power for local authorities to appoint Special Constables to help preserve the peace if they felt that existing police numbers were too low to cope. The Act gave Specials all the 'powers, authorities, advantages and immunities' of serving full-time constables and even allowed for a fine of 5s for any man who refused to serve if called on. On the other hand, it also granted for reasonable expenses to be paid when on duty. From the middle of the century special constables were sworn in on a semi-permanent basis to police the railway and canal construction industry, which was booming at the time. So the 1914 Act built on the existing service and at the end of August, Parliament heard that 'special constables are being enrolled as a volunteer force, consisting of persons who, being unable to undertake military service, are desirous of rendering useful service to their country in the maintenance of public order. In almost every case they have undertaken to serve without pay, but out-of-pocket expenses will in some cases, at any rate, be paid, and this House yesterday passed a Bill which will enable the police authority to grant them allowances in case of injury on duty.'

An account of one unit of special constables in London described a shift parading for duty: 'they were clad in every variety of overcoat and hat; some were armed with truncheons, some with walking sticks, and some were leading or being led by dogs.' The idea was to use Specials to guard 'vulnerable points' likely to be attacked by the roaming groups of German agents that rumours insisted were ready to rise up at any moment. In Wandsworth, the inspector sent his keen amateur policemen to guard a site he described as having 'an astonishing pungency' that regular officers refused to patrol.

Special Constables set out on patrol.

At first, Specials were provided with just an armband but as time went on a uniform was issued. So great was the contribution they made that in 1917 even the tight-fisted West Riding Standing Joint Committee agreed to spend £15-4s-6d on twenty-one new caps for Divisional Commanders and £25-10s on 120 silver badges for Sectional Commanders. Alderman Booth declared that he was not a great believer in what he called 'man millinery' but even he admitted 'these men were spending a lot of time on this work and devoting a lot of energy to it and under the circumstances he thought they might agree to the suggested purchases.'

The regular police force continued with the routine duties of law enforcement, investigating, for example, the suicide of a prisoner in Wakefield prison in September 1914 to avoid a flogging ordered by the prison's Visiting Committee as punishment for 'two very violent assaults upon warders.' Asked whether 'the Home Office is unable to devise some less degrading method of dealing with passionate and refractory prisoners?' the Home Secretary responded that the 'method of dealing with passionate and refractory prisoners is not free from difficulty, but as now advised I see no reason for reconsidering the law.' Punishment was intended to be swift and harsh, whatever the impact on the offender. In the years to come, the same attitude would spread to affect even the most law abiding citizens as they struggled to weave their way through a mass of wartime legislation that made it all but impossible not to break some law or other on a daily basis.

For the beleaguered police force, war brought a huge increase in workload at a time when trained officers were in short supply. As early as 6 August, the *Yorkshire Post* complained of panic buying of everything, including petrol, adding 'more than likely that the police will have something to say to motorists selfish enough to lay in stocks beyond their requirements.' The police, though, had more than enough on their hands without measuring the contents of petrol tanks. To the fears of German spies poisoning water supplies was added an order that all stackyards where harvested crops were stored were to be patrolled by a constable at night to prevent damage. According to the West Riding Standing Committee at County Hall, 'It was quite possible that a stack fire might be caused by some of the King's enemies who were unfortunately still allowed to reside in the United Kingdom'.

All police leave in August 1914 was cancelled as they struggled to keep control of the usual run of the mill pre-war offences and the sudden increase in criminal behaviour as more and more every day activities fell foul of a new piece of legislation which was passed almost unnoticed as an emergency measure a few days after the declaration of war. It began as a simple paragraph published in the *London Gazette*:

(1) His Majesty in Council has power during the continuance of the present war to issue regulations as to the powers and duties of the Admiralty and Army Council, and of the members of His Majesty's forces, and other persons acting in His behalf, for securing the public safety and the defence of the realm; and may, by such regulations, authorise the trial by courts martial and punishment of persons contravening any of the provisions of such regulations designed -

(a) To prevent persons communicating with the enemy or obtaining information for that purpose or any purpose calculated to jeopardise the success of the operations of any of His Majesty's forces or to assist the enemy; or

(b) To secure the safety of any means of communication, or of railways, docks or harbours; in like manner as if such persons were subject to military law and had on active service committed an offence under section 5 of the Army Act.
(2) This Act may be cited as the Defence of the Realm Act, 1914.

The Defence of the Realm Act – or DORA as it was generally known – was to govern the lives of every man, woman and child in the country for the next four years, granting draconian powers to control virtually all aspects of daily life. As Sir John Hammerton, editor of the wartime periodical *The Great War: The Standard History of the All-Europe Conflict,* explained:

In other words, the military authorities could arrest any persons they pleased and, after court martial, inflict any sentence on them short of death. In addition, the military authorities were allowed to demand the whole or part of the output of any factory or workshop they required. They were also allowed to take any land they needed. This, in effect, made the civil administration of the country entirely subservient to the military administration.

In the coming years, DORA would come to dominate British life. People could be arrested and even imprisoned for setting off fireworks, speaking in a foreign language on the telephone, owning pigeons without a licence or harming a pigeon that didn't belong to them. A man went to prison for sending a box of matches by post, another for buying his wife a drink. Whistling in the street meant a trip to court, as would feeding a slice of bread to the ducks in the park. DORA had, for example, made loitering near a railway bridge a criminal offence and a potentially dangerous one. At the end of the first week of war, the *Yorkshire Post* reported an incident in Newcastle when a man carrying an attache case approached a bridge and was challenged by an armed soldier. The man ran to a nearby boat and got in. The military patrol got into another and gave chase, eventually shooting the man who died from his wounds. In October, Mr J.S. Sanderson, of Clifton House, Ossett, wrote to the *Ossett Observer* claiming to have seen strange flashes in the sky over two nights. 'Are they,' he wondered, 'pre-arranged signals between members of the German Secret Service Corps?' The police were asked to investigate. Almost as a foretaste of anti-immigrant claims a century later, the West Riding Standing Joint Committee heard from the

Distress Committee about the risk of German spies hiding among the refugees flooding into the country and asked the police to take precautions. The Chairman replied that he thought that 'under existing war conditions the police had as much as they could do.' Having the police interrogate all refugees was going beyond their powers. The police, already struggling to put enough men on the beat to cover everything, politely pointed out that even if they did manage to intercept a group of plotters, armed with nothing more than truncheons there was not much they could do against armed agents. Meeting in Wakefield on 16 September, the Standing Committee for the West Riding agreed and put aside £1,255 for the purchase of revolvers, holsters and ammunition for the police. As Reverend L.B. Morris explained, this would help the police guard waterworks and other property from German agents, arguing it would be impossible for the police to defend themselves armed with 'nothing but walking sticks'.

Most annoying of all DORA's many rules for Wakefield folk were the ones governing where, when and with whom a man could drink. Concerns about alcoholism on a national level had been growing for years and were a particular problem in the industrial towns of the north. The Chancellor of the Exchequer, David Lloyd George, had led the campaign against what he saw as a national dependence on alcohol, claiming that Britain was 'fighting Germans, Austrians and Drink, and as far as I can see the greatest of these foes is Drink.' As a result, DORA immediately allowed for restrictions to be put in place to curb drinking by placing all pubs near naval dockyards, barracks and arms factories under the control of the military commander of the area. Before the war, pubs had been open for over 19 hours a day, from around 5.00am until half past midnight. Many men were used to going for a pint on the way to work but that was not always a good idea for munitions workers. DORA reduced opening hours to just twice a day at 12.00 noon to 2.30pm and 6.30 to 9.30pm. Over the next four years, Wakefield police would fight a cat and mouse battle with local landlords to enforce DORA's many alcohol related offences.

Regular reports of out of hours drinking appeared in the local papers, usually leading to hefty fines for offenders. Former Wakefield Trinity player Thomas Newbould, landlord of the Spotted Leopard, in January 1916 was summonsed after Inspector Dakin heard noise coming from the pub in the early hours of the morning. Climbing on the window so he could see inside, Dakin watched Newbould serve three men with drinks. 'Newbould at first denied having served beer, later he claimed them as lodgers and finally he said he had been a fool.' He was fined a massive £50 or faced three months in prison and each of the drinkers £10 or one month. In another incident later in the year, police went into the Cardigan Arms in West Ardsley. 'Two police officers in plain clothes entered the "best room" of the house about about 10.20. [Arthur Bedford, from Batley] was playing the piano, and behind an advertisement card on top of the instrument the police found two glasses of beer. One of the officers picked up a glass, and Bedford jumped up, saying "heigh, hold hard, that's mine". Then, turning around and recognising to whom he was speaking, he at once bolted through the door.' Bedford was fined £2 and pub landlord Walter Lammas £10. It was not just publicans. Joseph Stones, owner of an off licence in Normanton, was fined £2 or the option of a month in prison for 'selling beer to an amount exceeding the measure asked for.' He had served a customer with a 'long pull' pint that gave almost an extra 3 ounces of beer in what the magistrate condemned as 'a deliberate offence'.

DORA also put an end to the buying of rounds by making it illegal to order a drink for anyone else – the infamous 'no treating' rule. Under the rule, a man taking his wife out for the evening was not allowed to buy her a sherry under penalty of a fine, and questions were asked by delivery drivers about whether the ban extended to their mules, who had sometimes become used to having a pint as a treat during their rounds. As one driver put it, 'I've never seen one the worse for drink.' Undercover police officers regularly patrolled pubs to ensure that no-one ever bought a pint for someone else. In one case, a man was challenged at the bar when he was seen with three pints in front of him. Having claimed they were all his, the officer accepted his excuse – but stood alongside him until he had drunk all three of them.

Coming out of the pub at closing time, refreshed drinkers faced darkened streets and the occasional accident was reported. Fear of Zeppelin raids had led to the introduction of a blackout and the police were tasked to enforce it. The problem was that exactly what was expected was unclear. In April 1915, a motorist checked with a Barnsley police inspector that his headlights were properly covered before he set out on a journey to Leeds. Arriving in Wakefield, he was pulled over by a policeman who told him that his lights needed to be dimmed and actually turned out when passing through the city.

A short time later he was pulled over by another officer who told him 'your lights are out' and watched the driver relight his headlamps. Checking the policeman was happy, the motorist set off again only to be flagged down by a police inspector a few streets later because he thought the lights were now too bright. After explaining what had happened, the inspector decided the lights were 'passable'. Unfortunately, Wakefield policeman number four didn't agree, stopping the car again and telling him 'you can't pass me and go through to Leeds with lights like them there.' In desperation, the driver bought some gummed paper and used it to shield the lamps and finally made it to Leeds without further problems. His frustration was shared later in the year by a Sheffield cutlery manufacturer who was summonsed at Wakefield for having powerful headlights on his car. In a letter to the court, Percy Potter complained about 'the variation in the lighting orders in force in different districts, and went on to say "had we travelled without lights and run over the constable, who stepped in front of the car, nobody would have been to blame; it would have been simply a verdict of "accidental death". But as it would have cost more to bury the constable than to pay, I prefer to pay.' He was fined £5 including costs.

Chasing drinkers who lingered too long after closing, motorists who tried to drive at night, householders who showed lights at night, monitoring foreigners, protecting food and water supplies and a multitude of other wartime tasks had been added to a job that had been difficult enough to start with. It was about to get worse.

By 1917, German submarines were preying on merchant ships bringing food supplies to Britain and the campaign was being highly successful, especially in cutting off imports of such staples as wheat from America and Canada. As a result, food shortages became severe and, once again, DORA was invoked to bring in rationing and to prevent food waste. Allowing a slice of bread to go mouldy became a criminal offence and feeding bread to pets or livestock could land the offender in court for a severe fine or even imprisonment. A widely reported case highlighted how seriously food was taken and was watched with interest by the Yorkshire press: When Mrs Hobson of Sheffield died in 1918, her son William decided, apparently against his late mother's wishes, to throw what the Court later called 'the usual party' after the funeral and asked his brother-in-law, Albert Kramer, a local pork butcher, to cater for it. The party ended and everyone went home. A week later, William and Albert were arrested and charged under the Defence of the Realm Act with wasting bread. The story emerged in court: William's sister, Sarah Day, lived a few doors away from her mother and had refused to attend the party. There was what was described as 'a lot of bad blood' between them and, a week after the party, Mrs Day had gone to her mother's old home and allegedly found a loaf of bread that had gone mouldy. She immediately reported this to Inspector Thomas Toye of the Food Control Committee who visited the house and declared the loaf inedible and therefore wasted. It was enough to have both William and Albert arrested and potentially facing imprisonment but when the matter reached Sheffield Police Court in February, the case against Kramer was quickly dropped and the argument centred on whose bread it actually was. William insisted that when he left the house, he had looked around and there was no bread on the table. He also claimed that he did not know that his sister had a key. Unable to prove that Sarah had not placed the loaf in the house in order to get back at her brother, the magistrates gave up and dismissed the case, but trials for food wasting and hoarding were increasingly common as neighbour watched neighbour for signs that they had more than their fair share.

Often following reports from jealous fellow citizens, food hoarders were dragged before the courts by the police on behalf of the Food Control Committee. Wakefield seems to have managed better than many areas by not having its first case brought to court until December 1917 when Alice Wood, of Doncaster Road, was found to have over 27lbs of tea stored in her home along with 17lbs of sugar. It was, the magistrates decided, an amount 'exceeding the quantity required for ordinary use and consumption' by Mrs Wood, her husband and their daughter. Further prosecutions followed as the war dragged on with Carl Andrassy, a former pork butcher who had been forced out of his business at Keighley early in the war being fined £20 and costs for hoarding 17lbs of beef dripping. Elsewhere, John Preston, of Northgate, was charged under the Rabbit (Prices) Order for selling rabbits at 2s-3d instead of the 1s-9d fixed price allowed by law. He was sentenced to a fine of £10 or face two months in prison. Cases were brought over 'adulterated milk' that had been watered down and for sales of meat that was perhaps politely described as past its best. Even when not selling poor quality food or overcharging customers, shopkeepers needed to take care. George Mercer, of Horbury, was fined 19s-6d for selling a pie at 9.20pm in breach of a new 'Early Closing Order' introduced in October 1916, forcing shops to close at 8.00pm unless they were selling 'newly cooked' food. George's pies, although cooked that day, were deemed not to be 'provisions in a hot or nearly hot state' and meant 'for immediate consumption'. A test case in Bradford argued about whether tripe was 'newly cooked' after a judge bought some on his way home one evening. Another argued that cold cooked meats should be exempted. In Todmorden a shopkeeper argued that his pies had been cooked that day and so were 'newly cooked' but had a harder time convincing the court that his 'ice cake' counted as 'hot or nearly hot'.

As shopkeepers found their opening hours forcibly reduced, the law was also used to try to make others work harder since one of the problems facing production was absenteeism, common across all industries before and during the war. It was claimed that refitting naval ships actually slowed down once war was declared because there was plenty of overtime available and men could earn the equivalent of their weekly wage by working a few days over the weekend. Many then took advantage of the fact and took the rest of the week off. In response, the Ministry of Munitions set up special 'Munitions Courts' to try cases of absenteeism or poor discipline among essential war workers. Leeds and Sheffield both set up specific courts but Wakefield's cases were dealt with alongside criminal cases in the city courts.

In June 1915, Frank Townend and John Dale, both from Stanley, appeared to answer a charge of absenteeism from Kilner & Sons bottle manufacturers. It was said that the two men failed to arrive for work, leaving 'a man and two boys to play' as 173 dozen bottles were spoilt. Their employer wanted £4-8s from each of them to cover the losses they had caused. The bottles, it was argued, were needed to supply the army and the prosecution said that although the two men only worked five days a week and earned good money, they frequently failed to show up for work and went drinking instead. Both men claimed to have been ill but the court refused to accept their excuse, awarding compensation and 9s-6d in costs. The director of the firm said that he was already losing £100 a week because of the number of employees who had enlisted and the defendants knew it but 'yet they insisted on absenting themselves from work in order to go drinking.' Another case in October 1915, saw five men from Glasshoughton in Castleford summonsed to court for absenteeism and fined 32s each – the cost of the wages they would have earned. The court heard that in the first year of war alone Glasshoughton pit had already lost almost 1,000 men to the army and that production was badly affected. Since April, it was reported, of the 1,062 men employed at the pit, 375 had worked no more than four shifts per week and the mine had lost 37,363 working days through absenteeism running at 23 per cent of the workforce as opposed to the 5 per cent agreed as being a reasonable rate for all reasons. April saw shortages of coal in London and by the end of the year, domestic coal became rationed. The comments of the Yorkshire Miners Association were that the local men did not realise the national situation. Those who did were extremely worried.

By 1917, all charges such as 'Using Abusive Language' at work, 'Interfering with Other Workmen' and 'Losing Time' could attract a £1 fine as week after week the Munitions Court sat alongside the police courts and anyone deemed to not be pulling their weight could find themselves turned into a convicted criminal. Usually, these matters were dealt with at a local level but any offence under DORA could be tried by court martial and, in theory at least, if it was deemed that they were committed with the intention of helping the enemy, the penalty could be death. In reality, no cases ever went that far and few people believed they ever would, but the draconian measures of DORA allowed for it. DORA also attempted to determine how people should think. For a variety of reasons, not everyone fully supported the war. Strikes were as widespread as the offers to work over holidays to maintain production. For those with family serving overseas the behaviour of some trade unions was seen as self serving in the extreme. The Amalgamated Society of Engineers, for example, were openly mocked during their many strikes and it was claimed that sometimes not even those striking knew why they were out.

Trades Unions and leftist politicians had opposed the war from the outset but had largely muted their objections once the war started, but an active anti-war movement continued. They held protests and meetings and even set up an escape route for those attempting to avoid military service by fleeing to Ireland where the political situation meant that Conscription would not be enforced. Huddersfield and the surrounding area was considered by the government as 'a hotbed of pacifism' and Wakefield had its own share of dissenters. In July 1916, Normanton miner George Sharp was brought to Wakefield Court and charged under DORA with 'making a statement likely to prejudice recruiting, discipline or the administration of His Majesty's Forces.' Superintendent Jackson explained how George

Madley, a soldier who had enlisted in 1914 but who had later been discharged after losing an arm, had returned home from hospital recently. Sharp had asked how he was going on and when Madley told him 'I'm all right, I only lost a wing'. Sharp 'thereupon said, "What ******* good are you now? What do married men want to go for?" at the same time pointing to the empty sleeve. Madley replied, "to fight for single ones". Sharp then said "You were not forced to go" and on Madley remarking "No, I went to fight for my King and country", Sharp said "**** the King and country. What will the King and country do for you now?" A man named McHale came up and told Sharp he ought to be ashamed of himself and defendant and McHale then got to fighting.' Admitting he was the worse for beer, Sharp said he 'might have said a few words that were not right, but he was not a pro-German. He would have been willing to fight himself but he had a father and mother and two young brothers to keep'. With no fewer than nineteen previous convictions, Sharp was sentenced to a month's hard labour and ordered to pay £2-2s-6d or face a further month in jail. The bench, it was noted, 'thought he had been playing the game very low.'

With their fathers away, moral guardians worried about the growing levels of juvenile crime. A conference in Liverpool expressed concerns about the influence of cinema on young minds, leading cinema owners to argue that the issue should be taken up with the makers of 'questionable pictures' rather than blaming those who showed them. Censorship was considered but left to local authorities to decide what could or could not be shown in local picture houses. The rise in juvenile crime, cinema owners said, was 'solely to war conditions' and that cinemas had, in fact, done more to 'help the cause of temperance than all the restrictions of the Control Board.' In Huddersfield, a notorious group of youngsters formed themselves into the 'Clutching Hand Gang' and Wakefield, determined to clamp down on young offenders, began to hand out severe sentences. In November 1917, 13-year-old Willie Scarfe, of New Street, was hauled before the court. His father was away in Egypt and the court heard that young Willie was 'out of control'. After stealing 8s-4d from his mother, Willie went on a spree in Leeds, spending some of the money on 'pies and chocolates and finished up at a picture show'. He was found about midnight halfway between Leeds and Wakefield. He was committed to an Industrial School (a juvenile offender unit) until he was 16.

Child-related offences of a different kind were also increasingly common. It was an open secret that any woman finding herself 'in trouble' could find help at certain addresses in Leeds, but the help was illegal and potentially dangerous. In October 1915, an inquest opened on the death of Fanny Hill, the 36-year-old wife of boot repairer Abraham, of Streethouse. In the court was Jane Seggar from New Wortley in Leeds, arrested on suspicion 'of having performed an illegal operation'. Sarah Alton admitted she had given Fanny Seggar's name and address and was under the impression that Seggar was 'a lady doctor and that her husband was a medical man'. A verdict of 'wilful murder' was returned. Fortunately for Seggar, the murder charge was later reduced and, when the evidence was unclear when Mrs Hill actually developed the blood poisoning that killed her, she was acquitted.

Despite the number of men going overseas, violent crime continued to be a problem, sometimes for strange reasons. In June 1918, Harry Norton of Providence Street was fined £10 or told to face two months' custody for assaulting Roland Haigh, a mechanic working at the Vickers plant in Sheffield, and visiting his home on Albion Street for the weekend. On Saturday night, Haigh was walking home from Fieldhead when Norton suddenly accused him of being a German who had escaped from Lofthouse Camp. Despite Haigh's denial, Norton set about attacking him with his walking stick and breaking his glasses. Appearing in court, Norton pleaded guilty and his solicitor explained that 'he was under the impression that complainant was a German ... he had served in France, where he had lost an eye, and had been discharged from the army with a good character.' Exactly why he decided Haigh might be an escaped prisoner was never explained.

With ever more trivial crimes filling the courts and papers, from time to time serious crimes grabbed the headlines. On 10 August 1915, 24-year-old Barnsley miner Walter Marriott was hanged at Wakefield prison for the murder of his wife in June of that year. In December, hangman Henry Pierrepoint (father of the famous Albert Pierrepoint) returned for the executions of Harry Thompson on 22 December for the Honley murder of soldier's wife Alice Kaye, and again a week later for former army cook John McCartney for the murder of a woman in Pocklington. McCartney had the dubious distinction of being the last man to be executed in Wakefield gaol. Shortly afterwards, the prison was emptied to make room for the establishment of the Wakefield

Work Centre for Conscientious Objectors. It was argued that Wake-field prison could be used because there was now room because the crime rate had fallen.

Despite the national crisis, people carried on as they always had. Some good, some bad. As historian Gordon Corrigan has pointed out, the war may have taken the brightest and the best, but alongside them it also took wife beaters, child molesters, drug abusers and petty crooks. Crimes great and small were as much part of life in wartime Wakefield as they are today. No doubt some of those whose names appear in the court listings of the *Express* in the twenty-first century are the descendants of those whose names were there a hundred years ago, maintaining a family tradition of sorts. Finally, on the very last day of the war, Wakefield Court were sitting to hear the case of Emma Jane Parsons, of Normanton, who had refused to leave the grounds of Woodhouse Council School and used 'violent and abusive language'. In September, a teacher had 'chastised' her child for dis-obedience and Mrs Parsons went to the school saying she would 'wipe the floor with the thing that had struck her child' and shouted abuse at school staff. She was sentenced to a fine of 15s or seven days in jail. Life in Wakefield was getting back to normal ...

CHAPTER 8

Keep the Home Fires Burning

The Great War was a war of attrition. Put simply, whoever could outlast the other would win. For centuries, Britain had used its powerful Royal Navy to blockade its enemies, preventing food and war materials reaching them until they could no longer maintain their armies in the field but this time things would be different. Germany, too, had a powerful navy and in particular a fleet of submarines capable of roaming the seas almost at will. The English Channel, which had acted as a protective moat against invasion, was no barrier to Germany's airships or later to its 'Gotha' bombers, and British homes were no longer safe. For the first time, total war would create a new battlefield – the Home Front.

News of the outbreak of war was met with a nationwide spate of frantic buying. Prices rocketed as supplies dwindled and Leeds was reported to be gripped by what was almost a panic caused by the sudden rise in food prices. Alarmed by the thought of possible shortages, many people rushed heedlessly to buy more than they required of flour, bacon and other provisions. Thus a complete dislocation of supplies threatened until, after a day or two, the government regulated the position. There were the fears of unemployment, too; there were doubts as to the instant effect on commerce and industry; there were difficulties foreshadowed by the calling-up of men in the police force and in the various municipal services.

By the end of Wednesday, 5 August, the local shops had sold all their stocks of flour and some were still filled with shoppers 2 hours after normal closing time. Flour prices rose from 1s-11d to 2s-6d per stone in two days and bakers quickly passed on the price rise to their customers. Elsewhere, all other goods saw similar rises, with sugar leaping up by as much as 7d per pound in a few days (equivalent to a rise of over £2.20 in 2016). 'This rise', noted Sir John Hammerton, editor of the *Great War* periodical published throughout the war, 'fell most heavily on small and struggling retailers in poor districts, who could not afford to keep large stocks. As a result they had to increase prices for their customers, and the poorer classes were made to pay.' Soon, rumours of food riots and the looting of shops spread and the growing panic was only stopped by government intervention. After meeting with representatives of the large grocery firms and the Grocer's Federation, maximum retail prices were set for certain foods and a huge supply of sugar was compulsorily purchased by the government for sale at a fixed price.

Banks closed immediately to prevent a run on gold reserves and only re-opened on Friday to allow wages to be paid. Hasty legislation had been put in place to prevent individuals making large withdrawals and the papers all carried an announcement that 'banks re-opened and there was nothing in the nature of a panic ... The issue by the government of the £1 and 10s notes will be a big relief to the gold. The notes were issued in London yesterday and some were received by the Yorkshire Penny Bank from their head offices in London ... The alteration from coins to paper money will make no difference. The notes will be offered and accepted in payment just the same as gold and should be treated by the public with the same confidence. Wages paid in paper will have exactly the same purchasing power as if paid in gold and workers need have no hesitation in accepting them ... The new £1 notes are printed on small slips of paper 2½in by 5in. They bear the following wording printed in Old English type:

These notes are a legal tender for a payment of any amount. Issued by the Lords Commissioners of His Majesty's Treasury under authority of Act of Parliament

ONE POUND

(Sd) John Bradbury
Secretary to the Treasury

On the left hand side they bear the King's portrait amid ornamentation encircled by the inscription "Georgius V DG Britt Om Rex FD Ind Imp". The notes are printed on white paper, watermarked with the royal cipher.'

Businesses went on to short-time working and export orders were abandoned. Slowly, though, the situation settled and life began to get back to some sort of normality, but things would never be the same again. The early years of the twentieth century had seen a growing anti-immigrant feeling as thousands of people fled the oppressive regimes in eastern Europe. Those who could afford to had made the journey to a new life in America but many had settled in Britain. Very few towns were without at least one German pork butcher's shop and most had several. Mr Joynson-Hicks, MP for Brentford, already had something of a reputation for being anti-semitic, telling his Jewish hosts after his election to Parliament that he 'had beaten them all thoroughly and soundly and was no longer their servant.' In response to the outbreak of war, he turned his attention to the issue of how to deal with foreigners living in Britain: 'I do not move my Amendment with any hostility to the Germans in our midst. For many years England has been the home of foreigners, but I think they should be the first to realise that our first duty is to protect ourselves, and I would rather that irreparable damage should be done to any individual or individuals rather than our country should be placed in danger even for a moment. There are a very large number of aliens registered in this country at the present time. On the 9th September the Home Secretary gave us some figures, and he told us that there were 50,633 alien Germans registered in this country, and 16,014 Austrians. If we were to add 10 per cent. for non-registration up to that date, then we should get a total of over 73,000 alien enemies. I know it is a very difficult matter to say that A or B is a spy, nor could the German or the French say that A or B was a spy before they found him out. I think we are entitled to consider here what happened in the case of France and Belgium. There they have found a complete system of espionage. Soldiers, sailors, policemen, telephonists, tram drivers, professional men of every kind, and men of every class in the working life of France and, Belgium have turned out to be spies. Any officer or soldier who has returned from the front will tell you that those countries have been infested with spies. Now England is a greater enemy to Germany than either France or Belgium. The enmity of Germany is more directed against us at the present time and has been for some years past, than against Belgium or France ... On the other hand, England has been the easiest country to enter, and therefore it is fair to assume that as we are considered the greatest enemy of Germany and as ours is the easiest country to enter, we have a larger number of spies than either Belgium or France. You may say that this does not matter unless Germany invades us, but we must prepare for eventualities. Personally, I am not one of those who think that we shall be invaded, but we must prepare for eventualities. If there is no possibility of invasion, why is the Government providing against it? Why are trenches, wire entanglements and other reasonable precautions which sane men would take to protect us being prepared by our military advisers? I think those who are responsible for dealing with the spy question should take the same steps to protect the country against the possibility of trouble from spies as the military authorities are doing ... I have a return here, not of Germans who are registered to-day, but of Germans who were registered in the Census returns three years ago, and it shows a very small proportion of people registered then as Germans compared with the number of Germans we now find to be in the country. I think I am right in saying that in England and Wales alone there were only about 13,800 as given in the Census returns, whereas now we know that there are something like 56,000. Of that number an enormous proportion were in Kent, Sussex, Essex particularly, and Yorkshire – all those counties along the East Coast of England. Hon. Members may laugh, but why did those men go and settle there, unless it was with some intention of being useful to their own friends if and when the day came, possibly even of an invasion of Great Britain. The Home Secretary has always been an optimist. He dealt with this matter last Session in the most optimistic spirit. He told us that nobody had been shot.'

Newspapers encouraged their readers to check the papers of anyone claiming to be Swiss or whose accent sounded vaguely Germanic with the *Daily Mail* claiming that German agent waiters might poison soup or barbers might slit their customers throats. As the hysteria reached its peak, German Shepherd dogs became 'Alsatians' and German Measles was renamed 'Belgian Flush'. Assistants at Boots the chemist explained to customers that the eau de Cologne they sold was made in Britain and had nothing to do with the city. Dachshunds were attacked in the streets and allegedly even killed when mobs cited them as 'proof' that someone was a German agent. Lord Haldane, whose efforts to modernise the British army had done much to make it ready for war, came under a barrage of abuse in the press as a German sympathiser because his dog was named Kaiser.

Just a week after the outbreak of war, Bernard Desser, of Brook Street, was brought before magistrates for having failed to register. He had been living in England for twenty-eight years, six of them in Wakefield but found himself remanded in jail with bail refused. In

October, 23-year-old Carlisle man Hermann William Otto was sent to prison for three months for failing to register when the court decided that despite being born in England and 'having always considered himself an Englishman', he was, in fact, German. Under the terms of the 1870 Naturalization Act, any woman marrying a foreign national took on his nationality, as did their children. Overnight, hundreds of British-born people who had never travelled far beyond their own county found themselves foreigners in their own homes – or as rabble rousers called them, 'hunwives'. The situation was rectified by the British Nationality and Status of Aliens Act 1914 which became law in January 1915 and removed the automatic loss of status, but for a time even the children of naturalised British subjects might not be legally classified as British if they had not been included in the father's application for citizenship.

An editorial in *The Times* of 25 August told readers that 'many Germans still in London are unquestionably agents of the German government, however loose the tie may be … They had in their possession arms, wireless telegraph apparatus, aeroplane equipment, motor-cars, carrier pigeons and other material that might be useful to the belligerent … It has been remarked by the observant that German tradesmen's shops are frequently to be found in close proximity to vulnerable points in the chain of London's communications such as railway bridges … The German barber seems to have little time for sabotage. He is chiefly engaged in removing the "Kaiser" moustaches of his compatriots. They cannot, however, part with the evidences of their nationality altogether, for the tell-tale hair of the Teuton will show the world that new Smith is but old Schmidt writ small.' The issue was further complicated when Belgian refugees fleeing the fighting began arriving in Britain. Forced out of their homes, thousands of refugees had flooded westward and by the end of 1914 an estimated 250,000 had arrived at the port of Folkestone with around 16,000 arriving on 14 October 1914 alone. Soon, housing Belgian refugees became not just a valuable service, but in some areas almost a competitive sport as various committees and local worthies threw themselves into helping the 'plucky Belgians'.

Sandal was the first area to organise aid for the newcomers with a meeting in the Council School in early September to announce that two houses had been made available for refugees and asked local people for help in supporting them as Lady Kathleen Pilkington became president of the newly created Sandal Refugee Houses

Committee. A fortnight later, what was described as a 'magnificent' meeting took place in the Corn Exchange when a request was made to the people of other parts of Wakefield to help. The Bishop of Wakefield took on the role of chairman of the War Refugees Committee based in the 'War Refugees Office' at County Hall which also administered Sir John Horsfall's Belgian Refugee Fund. The first eighteen refugees arrived at Sandal Station on 31 September and were met by a substantial group including Lady Kathleen, the Bishop, and two Roman Catholic priests, Father Ruthven from St Austin's, Wakefield, and Father Inkamp from Normanton, before being taken in private cars to stay initially at Woodlands. They were followed on 17 October by another group destined for homes in Ossett and were led in a procession behind the Ossett Brass Band to the Queen Street Primitive Methodist Sunday School. Fortunately, a local Catholic priest, Father Ryan, had spent time in Belgium and was able to act as an interpreter as the group settled in to their new homes. By the end of the month, Ossett had taken in seventy-five Belgians, most of whom were living in the school but a few lodged with local families. By October 1914 there were 114 refugees in the Wakefield area, with most in Ossett and twenty-five in Horbury, with some, like Percy Tew, at Heath Hall, offering homes to entire families. In other cases,

Albion Street, home to Wakefield's first Belgian refugees.

houses were rented for them with volunteers providing furniture, clothing and financial support. A house in Albion Street was taken by the Wakefield Relief Committee with girls from the High School furnishing it and providing regular support for 'their' family.

For a time, housing a refugee was fashionable and some were treated almost as pets. Local people were urged not to buy drinks for them because Belgians were thought to be unable to cope with the strength of British beer and concerns were raised about their diet. After all, Belgians were known to eat horse meat and local councillors struggled with the question of whether to allow some butchers to sell it because there were fears it might be passed off as beef. After a time, the standard joke between those who had housed their charges was to ask, 'and how are your Belgian atrocities?' and even as early as October 1914 the problem of what to do with them in the long term was on the minds of some. George Ellison wrote to the papers asking if German-owned businesses should be required to pay for upkeep of the refugees and others argued that they should find work or that the men should join the army.

The refugees had sometimes been carefully picked. Belgium's mining communities had been badly affected and many pitworkers found themselves forced out of home by the fighting around the main coalfield areas, but unions in Britain had made it clear they would not be welcome if they tried to find work that could be done by a British miner. It was a tricky situation for the refugees to be in. On the one hand, their hosts soon became less enthusiastic about supporting the fit and healthy refugees financially when they were capable of working to support themselves, but at the same time they had been warned against taking jobs away from local people. Only after a great deal of debate was it agreed in December 1915 that 'no further objection is to be raised by the Miners' Federation of Great Britain to the employment of Belgians underground provided that they are practical miners, understand English and receive trade union rates of wages.' Others found work in the munitions industry and were able to support themselves.

As news came back from France of the disastrous retreat from Mons, men flocked to the recruiting stations. Thousands enlisted, flooding the army's training system but also emptying workplaces as young men, eager for adventure, joined up in droves. To try to manage the influx, army height and medical standards were increased, leaving hundreds of thousands of potential recruits with no option but to return home. Unfortunately, in the patriotic fervour sweeping the country, any military-age male not in uniform soon found himself accused of being a 'shirker'. An 'amusing, novel and forceful method of obtaining recruits for Lord Kitchener's army' was reported from the Kentish town of Deal, where on 2 September the Town Crier had announced the formation of the White Feather Brigade, a group dedicated to shaming young men into enlisting by handing out white feathers as a symbol of cowardice to any man wearing civilian clothes and soon young women were giving them to men on every street in the country.

Taken up with enthusiasm, the movement soon drew attention for the way young women had attempted to shame men just back from the war with serious wounds and on one occasion accused a man of cowardice the day after he had collected his gallantry medal from the King. In reality, there were many reasons why a young man might not be in uniform despite their best efforts to join up. Even a slight health problem could be a cause for rejection and, in industrial towns where poverty and malnutrition had left their mark, large numbers of potential recruits were simply not tall enough. There were other reasons, too. Specialist engineering and technical skills were needed in the war industries and so men who had enlisted were 'fetched back' to their day jobs, sometimes wearing their khaki uniforms to work. In Liverpool an entire battalion had been created by recruiting dockers who then went back to their normal work but as soldiers, and a similar battalion was formed in the KOYLI. To protect men who were more valuable at home than away in the forces, special 'war service' lapel badges were introduced by the government and soon employers began producing their own to try to ease the embarrassment many essential staff were being subjected to.

As tensions grew between those who had family serving and military-age men still at home, professional sportsmen found themselves at the centre of a growing argument. Was it right that fit young men were playing or watching games while their contemporaries were fighting for the country's survival? Some believed that all professional sports should be cancelled immediately, others that they were 'a national necessity', vital for maintaining morale at home and in keeping with the government's insistence that people should carry on as normal. Cricket and racing, both in mid-season in August 1914, were the first to come under criticism but both argued that they were contractually obliged to continue for the time being. By 1914,

Skilled workers were sometimes brought back to their old jobs to ensure vital military components could be produced.

professional sports were big business and the Football Association fought hard on behalf of its members to argue that matches were ideal recruitment venues and so serving a useful purpose – itself supporting the view of opponents that footballers ought to set an example, not leave it to others to go in their place. Rules were hastily consulted and changed to allow players who did join to play for their units and even their clubs if they were based nearby but also to allow players to sign back up for their clubs after discharge from the army or navy, both previously forbidden.

The Yorkshire Rugby Union recommended that matches should be stopped in the county for the duration of the war but J.B. Cooke, Wakefield Trinity's representative at the meeting argued, 'It seems to me far better that the ordinary course be followed rather than the programme abandoned, more especially because of the effect on the public at large. The fact that so many have already volunteered for service is some evidence that the great bulk of players are prepared to do their duty and if others are required they will be in far better trim when wanted if they continue to play the game.' Gates fell as men enlisted and by the end of the year, attendance at Trinity matches were half what would normally be expected. By the end of the season, 1,500 players of the Northern Union had enlisted, including Trinity's captain, William Beattie, who had joined the KOYLI. When Beattie and Ernest Parkin returned to the side whilst on leave, officers of regiment appeared at the ground to recruit men.

After the controversial 'Khaki Cup' final between Sheffield United and Chelsea on 24 April 1915, professional soccer ended for the duration of the war. From then on, amateur matches were played and a very successful league of women players formed, but soccer players would no longer be paid anything more than basic expenses. In rugby, the decision to end competition lasted for a time but resumed for the 1916–17 season on the grounds that conscription had been introduced, and so both players and spectators were all men the army didn't need. By then, Trinity were struggling with a £750 mortgage on their grounds and an income so low it barely covered expenses. Mid-season it was announced that William Beattie had been killed in action.

From the start, the government had urged people to carry on as normally as possible. For local authorities that meant managing the already complex task of running a city whilst having their resources cut repeatedly. A great deal of responsibility fell on the shoulders of the corporation and especially the mayor, who was regarded as the town's first citizen and chief magistrate and as such was expected to take the lead in the seemingly unending variety of extra committees needed to maintain it on a war footing. John William Saville, a Conservative who had been a councillor since 1898 and had been made an alderman in 1907, was in post when war broke out and it fell to him to head the various recruiting and fund raising campaigns that sprang up everywhere. It also fell to him to ensure that Wakefield ratepayers were not out of pocket because of the war. At a time when war news was scarce, the mayor was occupied with a complaint from the Cattle Market Committee on 2 September 1914 when the Market Superintendent reported that on 13 August a military column with horses, guns and ammunition were billeted in the market and the calf sheds and that some damage was done to the pens in the sheds. The superintendent was asked to assess the damage so a claim for compensation could be made. Two weeks later there was a need to find substitutes for the two masters at Queen Elizabeth Grammar who had enlisted, and an agreement was made to pay serving masters the difference between their army pay and their salary as teachers and to reemploy them on return at least at the salary they had on volunteering. Within weeks, he had overseen the huge recruiting rallies around the district and arranged for room to be provided at County Hall for various relief agencies providing support to the hospitals, soldiers and their families, Belgian refugees and a host of others. All fitted around the everyday issues of local government.

'Flag Days' became an increasingly common event as charity collectors, or 'coppersnatchers' as they became known, pinned small paper flags to the lapels of anyone who donated to causes ranging from Serbian relief to a Belgian hospital or for Wakefield Prisoners of War. On one occasion no fewer than 800 collectors took to the streets of Leeds to raise money for the RSPCA's work with horses in use at the front. Although these collections raised thousands of pounds, in February 1917 the West Riding Standing Joint Committee met at Wakefield and proposed regulating flag day collections because of the 'enormous amount of fraud that has gone on, not only under flag days but under cover of charitable contributions for war purposes by ill-disposed people who pocketed the greater part of the money.' From then on, all collections would need to obtain the permission of the Chief Constable.

Most, of course, were genuine. The Wakefield Wesleyan Methodist Circuit provided a Buick motor ambulance which could carry four stretchers (or 'lying men' as the editor of the church magazine called them). They heard in August 1916 from a Methodist chaplain writing from the Somme that their vehicle was wearing well, despite heavy service. In July 1915 another ambulance, funded by Wakefield people in general and with Wakefield City inscribed on its side, was given to the Red Cross Society to take to France. Cigarettes were regarded as a necessity for men on active service and a collection at the Electric Theatre raised enough for 13,200 cigarettes and 5lbs of tobacco. In June 1915 Alice Fearn, aged of 30, was living with her widowed father in Wentworth Terrace, and began collecting money from her friends. Soon a committee was formed under the control of Mrs Haselgrave, wife of Lieutenant Colonel John Henry Haselgrave, the commanding officer of the Wakefield-based 1/4 Battalion of the KOYLI. By then they were able to supply up to 11,600 cigarettes and 3lb tobacco per week and noted that the men asked especially for Woodbines.

Another group of women gathered heather from the moors to be made up into sprays for buttonholes by children at Clarendon Street and Ings Road Schools and sold by them in the streets. The venture raised £60 for the cigarette fund which, by then was large enough to extend to include other KOYLI battalions. In March 1916 Lieutenant Colonel P. Kelly of the 6th battalion wrote to thank the women for consignment of 9,000 cigarettes received when the men were in 'some very wet and particularly uncomfortable' trenches. It was surprising, he said, how many men claimed to be from the 'Merrie Citie' when 'smokes' were handed out. From 1915, Wakefield Women's Working League met regularly in the Zion Chapel assembly rooms in George Street to make articles of warm clothing for men on the hospital ship HMS *Egmont* and in addition to scarves, mittens and shirts, they sent packages of sweets and chocolate. Similar groups met at other churches and chapels with the Unitarians establishing a Knitting Circle of older girls from Sunday School who met on Tuesday evenings and Saturday afternoons to make socks, belts, scarves and other items for local soldiers, using yarn provided by Mrs Haselgrave and other benefactors.

Anxious to maintain morale among all their troops, the military authorities became concerned that some men received plentiful parcels of socks, shirts, tobacco and sweets whilst others, who had no benevolent home town, received none. Gradually a system was established with collection depots in each area and all the individuals and groups engaged in making or buying items were asked to send them to these depots. From there, they were sent to 'comforts pools' in every theatre of the war. The Director General of wartime voluntary organisations, Sir Edward Ward, explained to Wakefield's mayoress that officers from any unit could then make their men's needs known and would receive a prompt response. Inevitably, as time went on, a combination of compassion fatigue and shortages of just about everything meant that donations began to wane. In January 1916, the Unitarian chapel's knitting circle produced six pillow cases and three pairs of bedsocks to VAD hospital along with five pairs socks, four balaclava helmets and four pairs of mittens, given to Mrs Haselgrave for KOYLI. That November, chapel minutes recorded 'There have been retiring collections since last Sunday in October to provide gifts for the chapel men in the army and navy. Only two guineas so far. Not nearly enough.'

Life went on as normally as possible. In November 1914, A.C. Snawston-Thomas, of Leeds, married Louise Firth at St Andrew's Church 'quietly, because of the war' during a 48-hour leave pass from his Doncaster-based Field Ambulance unit. As they prepared to go abroad, hundreds of young men hurriedly married their sweethearts and in December 1915, after a year of bad news, newspapers around the world seized on an item in the *Daily Mirror* of 27 December announcing the fairy tale story of the secret marriage in October of Rowland Winn, heir to Nostell Priory, to 'one of the most beautiful and charming chorus girls on the London stage', Eva Carew, and boasting that 'not even the bridegroom's nearest relatives were aware of the romance and will probably learn of it for the first time this morning.'

Rowland, serving with the Coldstream Guards, had obtained a special licence for them to marry at St Saviour's Church in Paddington, but the wedding was a near disaster. Firstly the best man, Captain Wentworth of the Royal Flying Corps, was planning to fly to London from his home defence base but was delayed and couldn't make it in time. Next, after waiting 25 minutes for the couple to arrive the vicar decided they'd changed their minds. The couple, 'smiling and happy', arrived to find he had left a few minutes before. Fortunately, the vestry clerk was still there. He leapt into Rowland's car to search for someone to perform the ceremony and found the Reverend

Nellie Green, aka Eva Carew, showgirl turned society lady.

G.S. Clarke, who agreed to officiate. Despite the *Mirror's* claims, the wedding was witnessed by Rowland's father ('Occupation: Peer of the Realm') and Eva – married under her real name of Nellie Green – was escorted by her father Charles (Occupation: 'Gentleman'). In fact, Charles was a restaurant manager and her sister was married to a miner, making Nellie of a very different social class to that of her new husband. Such weddings were not unknown and indeed the year before Earl Cowley had married actress Mae Pickard, and 1913 had seen no fewer than three peers, Lord Paget, the Duke of Leinster and Viscount Dunsford marry showgirls – but Rowland was making a very big decision by taking her for his wife.

Shortly after Lord Victor Paget married Olive May, a damning article appeared in *The Throne* (unofficial journal of the royal household), explaining the need for the aristocracy to 'Prevent Hereditary Peers from Debasing Their Blood.' According to the writer, 'the very existence of the lords as anything but a mockery and a laughing stock – is threatened by a development of recent years which every day grows to greater and more menacing proportions. We refer to the increasing number of unions between hereditary peers and ladies of inferior station – mesalliances which strike at the very heart of the whole reason d'etre of the House of Lords.'

On the one hand telling readers 'we have nothing to say personally derogatory to any of these ladies. On the contrary, we congratulate them most heartily upon the enterprise and ability that has enabled them to rise above the status of life to which they were born.' That said, it went on, 'that you cannot make a silk purse out of a sow's ear is a principle that has been admitted since the earliest times . . . Pure blood is always a most salient factor in the selection of leaders of men, and has been so recognized all through history. And in the case of hereditary peerages which entitle the holders to a seat in the House of Lords, it is not merely a valuable qualification, but the sole valid one. Therefore the peer who has sullied the blood of his family and of his descendants should be ipso facto debarred, him and his heirs, from sitting in the Lords'. In other words, Rowland was risking his entire future and bringing shame to his family by marrying his 'uncommonly beautiful' new wife. A ban on actresses at Court meant his new wife could never accompany him to the formal royal events which he, as an officer in the Brigade of Guards would be expected to attend and so he resigned his commission in order to join his friend Captain Wentworth in the Royal Flying Corps, completing his training and being promoted to Captain by mid-1916.

Stories about the couple, even today, claim that the family only learned of the secret marriage when the *Daily Mirror* broke the story eight weeks later and the *Yorkshire Evening Post* of 28 December 1915 declared that the only witnesses had been the vicar and the vestry clerk. Given the party his father had thrown for him just a year earlier, it seems Rowland could do no wrong in his parents' eyes. The couple's marriage certificate shows that Rowland's father, at least, attended the wedding and signed the certificate as a witness. Writing home from France, Rowland thanked his father, saying 'Eve' had told him that his parents had been 'extremely nice' to her whilst he was away and expressing his hopes that they would get to know her, as he did, as 'the most loveable person'. By the time Rowland completed his flight training, Eve was pregnant with the first of two sons and living in a London town house paid for by Lord and Lady St Oswald as a sign of their acceptance of their new daughter-in-law.

The story brightened a dark time. Germany had launched total war and December 1914 had seen their ships bombarding English coastal towns. Harold Sunderland, manager of the Public Benefit Boot Company in Hartlepool was wounded by a shell splinter when his shop was destroyed. Like hundreds of other residents, he and his family fled inland, taking shelter with his father-in-law in Wakefield where they became the centre of attention for a time. As fears of a seaborne invasion gradually faded, though, a new and more terrifying threat emerged that would bring the war to Britain's streets. On the night of 6–7 June 1915, a Zeppelin airship designated the L9 crossed the Yorkshire coast near Holderness and in just 13 minutes unleashed bombs on the city of Hull that left twenty-four people dead and forty injured. Censors prohibited the reporting of raids claiming that German intelligence could gather useful information that would help them in the future. As a result, the *Hull Daily Mail* carried no direct references to the attack, although that something had happened is clear from close reading of the papers over the following week when adverts appeared offering shelter from future raids: 'Zeppelin Raids – Bomb Proof Shelter. Use for one year, one person £5. F. Singleton & Co., 3 Alfred Gelder St, Hull.' There was anger in the city that there were no real defences against air attack and only a dummy wooden gun guarded by a single soldier mounted on the roof of the Rose, Down & Thompson munitions factory. Public anger spilled over into an attack on a Royal Flying Corps truck and stones thrown at an RFC officer in Beverley. Wakefield had even fewer defences.

Long-range air navigation was still in its infancy and the Zeppelin raiders were often lost. When Bolton and Sheffield were bombed later in the war, the crews reported having hit their designated targets of Derby and Lincoln but the Humber estuary, pointing like a finger to

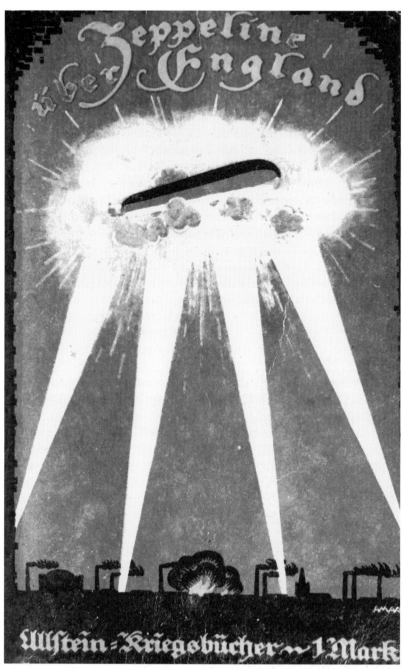

'Zeppelins Over England', a 1916 German account of the air war. The book contained a long list of towns supposedly hit by bombing raids, but with air navigation in its infancy, most were just guesses as to where the bombs may have fallen.

the industrial centres of the West Riding, put Wakefield under the path of the giant airships as they crossed the coast. Blackout restrictions were strictly enforced and new laws under the Defence of the Realm Act had made bonfires and fireworks illegal, to prevent signals being sent to attackers. Whistling in the street during an alert became a criminal offence in case the crews high above could hear it over the noise of the wind and their engines. At first, the Zeppelins seemed invincible. They flew so high that by the time observers had spotted them and home defence fighters had climbed to the right height they were long gone. Even if they could catch them, the British aircraft lacked the right weapons to do any real damage. Tactics included dropping bombs onto the airship or even an anchor, which was then towed along to try to tear open the fuselage. It was not until 1916 that explosive bullets were made available and soon the tide began to turn.

Known to the locals around his family home at The Grange, in Ackworth, as 'Billy', Lieutenant Wulstan Joseph Tempest, of No. 39 Squadron was one of five brothers serving in the war. When Zeppelin L31 appeared over London Tempest spotted it and gave chase, even

Kapitanleutnant Frankenburg, commander of the Zeppelin that bombed Sharlston.

though he was struggling with a fault in his aircraft that meant he needed to keep hand pumping a lever to maintain pressure in his fuel tanks as he flew towards the enemy. The situation was not helped by 'a very inferno' of anti-aircraft fire coming from London's defences buffeting his frail plane. Trying to keep pumping his fuel lever, fly the aircraft and fire his guns at the same time, Tempest closed in on the L31. 'I let her have another burst as I passed under her tail', he later reported, 'and flying along underneath her pumped lead into her for all I was worth ... As I was firing I noticed her begin to go red inside like an enormous Chinese lantern and then a flame shot out of the front of her and I realised she was on fire. She then shot up about 200ft, paused, and came roaring down straight onto me before I had time to get out of the way. I nose dived for all I was worth with the Zepp tearing after me, and expected every minute to be engulfed in the flames. I put my machine into a spin and just managed to corkscrew out of the way as she shot past me roaring like a furnace.' Tempest instantly became a national hero.

Despite mounting losses, the Zeppelins kept coming. At about 9.00pm on 27 November 1916, airship L21 crossed the coast near Atwick and headed inland as part of a large raiding force. She was spotted over Driffield at about 9.45pm and continued on a meandering course inland. Censorship at the time prevented newspapers reporting on the effects of raids so that the enemy could not know whether they had hit the right target but the *Pontefract and Castleford Express* of 1 December 1916 managed to provide a detailed account of L21's visit that somehow managed to pass the censors by, writing about '... a Northern Town known far and wide for several possessions comprising ancient and medieval buildings, a public park etc., etc., etc. In all it's long history the town which has borne the shocks and blows enough had not hitherto been the object of attention of these modern murder machines, the Zepp, although more than once like engines have passed over the old Borough elsewhere on wicked slaughter bent, so that Monday night's visitation was at once a novel and altogether alarming experience. The first intimation of the presence of Zepps in the district was assumed when the public gas supply was turned very low at about 9.15pm. At about 10.30pm the doubts of most people were determined by the distant booms of bursting bombs. Then of course everybody began to be interested. Meantime the 'specials' were discharging their duty in a way that does them exceeding credit. At this time it was thought that the effort of destruction was aimed at distant munition works or at some large centre of population, but when at about 11 o'clock there were terrific explosions and loud reports accompanied by heavy gun shooting none needed to be told that at last the huns were upon them. As a matter of fact, proved next morning by many witnesses, one or more of the terrible visitants hovered over the town and the neighbourhood for a considerable time, dealing out had they been accurately aimed, sufficient bombs to destroy half the town and many of the dwellers therein, not to speak of several big villages at some distance ... It was at this time that the effects of the explosions and the shooting were most telling making the windows of old properties rattle, smashing some, and rousing the townsfolk, the people of the countryside, and the villagers generally. There is no need to say that many persons were scared, that many remained calm and cool, and that a large number of people risked going into the open to see the unwanted sight – a raider airship hovering, droning, throbbing with inward forces and threatening everybody and everything beneath it ... About 11 o'clock the shooting and bombing explosions, near or distant, became less frequent and shortly afterwards the droning gradually died away in the distance. Those who had taken refuge in basements etc came out to learn what could be learnt and others retired to their beds. The visitation was not ended however for at about 11.30 the unwelcome sound of distant bombs was heard and in an amazingly short time bombs exploded quite near and the droning was again practically overhead accompanied by what sounded like cracks of "heavens artillery" terrific and nerve shaking to quiet peaceable people. The experience however did not last long and about 11.45 the visitors cleared off for good although explosions were heard in the distance, either of their making or the shots of airmen in pursuit. For the space of an hour or more there were many people in the streets curious to see all and learn all they might and some especially where children were concerned remained in what they thought to be safe places. Upon the whole it may be said that the townsfolk behaved bravely and that the 'specials' did their duty as brave folk would expect them to do it. Next morning was given up by large numbers of people to investigation and gossip in regard to the visitation. Many persons without a doubt saw the Zepp, possibly two ... That thousands of people on Tuesday and Wednesday and since have inspected these evidences of the nocturnal visit needs scarcely be stated. Hundreds have carried off souvenirs of the occasion in the form of bits of shrapnel etc. The prevailing feeling is astonishment – that the town should be thought worthy of attention and that so marvellous an escape from harm has been the townsfolk's portion. As regards certain villages not far distant we find that eleven or twelve bombs of both kinds were dropped. Five explosions fell into waste heaps, two incendiaries struck the ground close to an old residence, an incendiary which did not explode found its billet in a field and three incendiaries dived into an immense waste pile. In no instance was any damage of note done, no building was struck, and no person was seriously injured. Marvellous is the only word that fits the circumstances.'

There were no direct casualties but the paper went on to report that 'On Thursday afternoon an inquest was held in a little northern

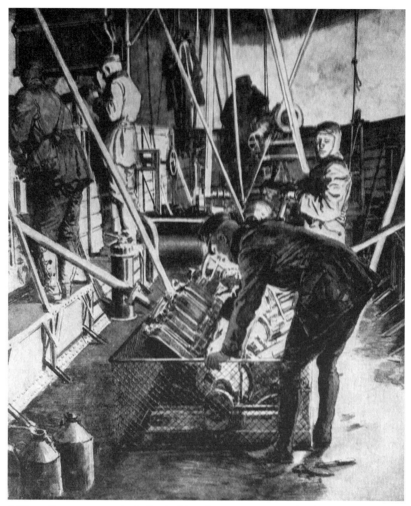

A Zeppelin crew prepares its load of bombs.

village on the body of a woman who died from shock during the raid. The woman, who was 49 years of age, had for some time past been suffering from heart trouble, for which she had been attended by a doctor. When the alarm was given on Monday night she along with other women and some children sought safety in a cellar in a garden near her home. She got over the shock of the first visit all right but when on the return journey an airship dropped an explosive bomb within 300 yards of her home she fainted and died in the arms of a neighbour a few minutes later. Although bombs were dropping all round the countryside, the deceased's daughter bravely set out on her cycle through very lonely country to fetch a doctor, but her mother had passed away before the doctor arrived. The coroner expressed his deep sympathy with the husband and family and later in summing up the evidence, said that the poor woman's death was directly due to the murderous barbarity of the enemy, that it was a disgusting and cruel shame. The jury unanimously returned the following verdict: "Died from shock due to fright owing to bombs dropped by an enemy airship near her home."'

Having bombed Pontefract Park, the Zeppelin continued towards Leeds. After the war, a history of Leeds explained: 'Another occasion when a Zeppelin airship came anywhere near Leeds – the night of Monday, November 27th, 1916 – its presence was made known by the sound of bombs dropped indiscriminately in Pontefract Park, 12 miles away, and the dull boom of the explosions was heard plainly on the north side of Leeds. The warning [was] given to the city. . . and many people spending the evening in town had scarcely reached their homes on the outskirts when, just at the hour of midnight, the explosions broke the silence of the night. It was not known until next day – and then only through gossip locally – that the alarm was caused by two Zeppelins which had been careering around the Barnsley district and were making their way back to the coast. One airship went off in the direction of Ferrybridge, and the other in a more northerly direction, passing over the V.A.D. hospital at Ledston Hall, and creating a diversion for the convalescent soldiers, many of whom turned out of bed to see all that was to be seen . . .' ' We can never, of course, know what was in the mind of the officer in charge of the bomb dropping gear,' wrote a *Yorkshire Post* correspondent afterwards. 'He may have thought that he was over some of the big works of Leeds – only about 10 miles away – or he may merely have been in a hurry to finish his work and get home to breakfast. At any rate, in quick succession he rained incendiary bombs upon the unoffending turf of Harewood Park; and when day broke most of these were pulled up out of the damp soil like ripe turnips and formed a most interesting exhibition in the coach-house of the Harewood Arms. At the time, it was suggested that the commander of the Zeppelin knew more than he was generally credited with, and that in dropping these bombs he was merely endeavouring to carry out the principles of Applied Kultur,

Harewood House being then in use as a Red Cross Hospital. The Germans probably knew that it was not defended by anti-aircraft guns, as were the arsenals of Leeds." Having successfully disturbed the turf in the Park, and, by then, having only a few more bombs left, the raider turned eastwards for home. He may or may not have been able to see the houses of the hamlet. At any rate, as he was crossing the main road near to the principal gates of the Park, he dropped another incendiary bomb. This fell on the corner of the roof of a cottage, but with such ill-luck from the enemy's point of view that on going through the tiles it sank into the water cistern, and was immediately extinguished. The impact of the falling bomb destroyed the cistern and flooded the bedroom below, but such damage can hardly be said to be worth even the cost of the bomb. The Zeppelin's farewell to Harewood was another incendiary bomb which dropped into an empty hen-house belonging to Dr. Matthews." "Over the line of Harewood Avenue, the Zeppelin came within view of the anti-aircraft gun station between East Keswick and Collingham, was picked up by the seachlight, and was fired upon, though without result. By way of acknowledgment the Zeppelin dropped its last two incendiary bombs,

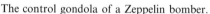

The control gondola of a Zeppelin bomber.

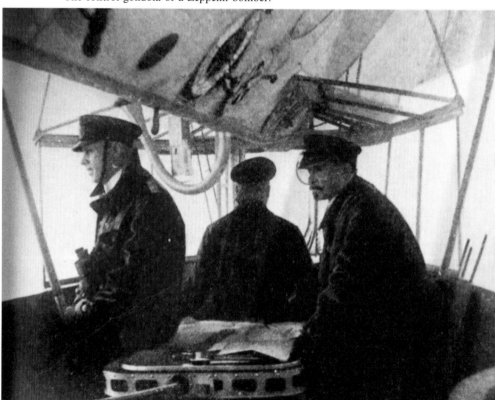

both of which fell in the field in which the gun was placed. An incend-iary bomb dropping into a soft, damp meadow is not a very terrify-ing thing, and here, again, beyond a couple of holes in the turf, the Germans achieved nothing. Perhaps the greatest things that they might claim for their enterprise were that they had dropped quite a large weight of bombs on the estate of the Lord Lieutenant, the repre-sentative of the King in the West Riding, and had avoided running any very great risk themselves. That Leeds escaped was the more remarkable because on the same night a fire broke out at the Kirby Banks Screw Works, near Meadow Lane, and although soon sub-dued, was at its brightest when the Zeppelin was hovering over Wharfedale. It was, indeed, the flares which had been lit in Pontefract Park, to guide our aeroplanes there, that attracted so much attention in that particular neighbourhood. The night was exceedingly still; the sky was clear and star-lit; but the darkness which had been system-atised all over the city ensured protection.'

The airship wandered on, first towards Leeds where anti-aircraft fire forced her to turn south until she reached the outskirts of Wakefield, dropping a high explosive and two incendiary bombs on Sharlston. The blackout was in force and the population had been warned by the lowering of gas pressure by the local corporation which meant gas lamps in homes across the borough went out. Already their colleagues aboard the L16 had passed overhead without dropping any bombs as it circled high above Wakefield and Barnsley before drop-ping its bombs randomly across the county. Now Kapitanleutnant Frankenburg, commander of the L21 and one of Germany's most experienced bomber crewmen was lost. The bombs were not aimed at any particular target and very little damage was done before the ship passed on, flying over the Peak District and over Macclesfield before bombing towns in the Staffordshire potteries. His ship was later shot down off the coast of Yarmouth and crashed into the sea. There were no survivors.

In comparison to what was to come a generation later, the Zeppelin raids were little more than a nuisance but for a nation that had believed itself to be protected by the English Channel and the might of the Royal Navy, the threat of being attacked in their own homes brought shockwaves of terror through the population. The merest hint of a Zeppelin raid brought production in factories to a halt as workers fled to open countryside, believing that to be safer, although the German bombs fell more often into empty countryside than onto real targets. For both sides, this was a war of attrition. It was a war where destroying the enemy's ability to fight was every bit as important than destroying his army. The aim of the raids was to create terror. If panic could be created among war workers then production would fall, as it did every time a raid or even a false alarm was reported. When Sheffield was bombed in September, hundreds of people had fled and wild tales of a city ablaze had spread. For nights afterward, families hiked out into the countryside to sleep in what they thought would be relative safety. Wakefield reacted with a mixture of bemusement and anxiety to its own near miss.

By the end of 1916, German submarines were targeting merchant ships at a rate of 100 per month. Heavily dependent on imports, Britain was facing starvation. Wheat was in short supply and the Ministry of Food issued a leaflet explaining: 'I am a slice of bread. I measure 3 inches by 2½ and my thickness is half-an-inch. My weight is exactly an ounce. I am wasted once a day by 48,000,000 people of Britain ... When you throw me away or waste me you are adding twenty submarines to the German Navy'. The Defence of the Realm Act was once again brought in to make wasting bread a criminal offence. Overnight, feeding ducks in the local park could lead to a jail sentence. 'We must all eat less food,' said the Ministry of Food, 'especially we must all eat less bread and none of it must be wasted. The enemy is trying to take away our daily bread. He is sinking our wheat ships. If he succeeds in starving us our soldiers will have died in vain.'

Some areas had already introduced voluntary rationing schemes but, as Dorothy Peel recalled, the problem of

Families were encouraged to cut back on everything.

Before you light a fire THINK

Think of the men fighting in the sodden trenches. Think of the Italian soldiers in the snow. Think of the wounded in hospital. Think of someone fighting who is very dear to you. Remember that the more coal for you the less coal for them. The see if you cannot do without the fire you meant to light. Follow the rule, one family one fire. The day you have a fire in the kitchen—sit in the kitchen. You can only burn your coal once. Every fire you save now you will be glad of later on.

Put off lighting the fire as long as you can—and put it out immediately you have done with it.

The coal you are going without is forging the key to VICTORY

Issued by the Coal Mines Dept., Board of Trade, Holborn Viaduct, E.C.1.

feeding a family was becoming serious. 'The conduct of certain tradespeople who at this time shut their shops to the general public and sent out meat and other goods to favoured customers via the back door infuriated the people and occasionally the luckless butcher boys were held up and the contents of their basket looted. The knowledge that some well-to-do folk were hoarding food also caused discontent. It was these annoyances which made local authorities adopt rationing schemes before national compulsory rationing came into force.' A major campaign was launched to get people to eat less and reduce waste. Public lectures were given on how to produce meals for 4d a day and recipes for loaves made from rice, maize and pearl

Local schemes encouraged people to use even less than the government ration.

barley were circulated as local schoolchildren sang 'Each Loaf Saved Drives a Big, Long Nail'. Elsie McIntyre, a munitions worker in Leeds, later recalled:'The most awful thing was food, it was very scarce. As we are coming shift, someone would say, 'There is a bit of steak at the butcher's.' And I would get off the train and then go on the tram and I'd get off at Burley Road and run to the shop. Only to find a long queue and by it got to my turn there would be no more meat, only half-a-pound of sausage. You see, that's coming off night shifts, you went straight into a queue before you could go to bed. Then my mother would be in home needing half a stone of flour for the kids, you see. We were lucky if we got up to bed by 11.00am and up again at four to catch the train, five o'clock to Barnbow.'

Finding enough to eat became the focus of everyone's attention and queueing became part of daily life. 'We had the ration books', recalled H. Middleton, 'and we all used to stand in the queues for cigarettes, meat and what have you. If we were walking up the road and saw a queue at a shop we used to stand in it . . . to see what they'd got and whatever it was we used to get some'. Schools reported a growing problem with absenteeism as children were sent to wait for hours in long queues for whatever rationed items could be found. Maud Cox, aged eight in 1917, remembered 'Mum took me up there and put me in the queue and she says, "Now stand still and don't move until I get the other ones away to school and I'll come back. But keep my place". Of course I was standing there and the snow was deep, it was right up over your feet. The next thing I knew, I was lying on a bench in the dairy. I'd fainted.'

Charged with the task of maintaining food supplies, the West Riding War Agricultural Committee began sitting at County Hall in November 1915 and opened by discussing the use of 12 and 13-year-olds as farm labour and the possibility of releasing older children from school and work to stay at home and look after their younger brothers and sisters so their mothers could find full-time work. After the army had taken all available horses, the committee arranged for some to be loaned back for farm work and in early 1916, soldiers from nearby training camps were sent to help with ploughing. At the same time, the Education Committee gave permission for boys and girls between 12 and 14 to be released from school to work on farms or to let their mothers go to work whilst they provided childcare. Plans for convalescent soldiers from Wakefield's auxiliary hospitals to be brought in as labourers were also considered.

School attendances fell as children were kept away to wait in the many queues a shopping trip required.

In May, British Summer Time was introduced to allow extra working time on the land and provision was made for the training of around fifty women workers found by Lady Catherine Milnes-Gaskell. Conscription was threatening farmers as much as anyone and limits were put forward: A farm should have one man per fifteen cows if there were women or boys to help. One man would be needed per 100 sheep or one labourer per 100 acres. As more and more men were conscripted, the limit was raised to one man per twenty cows and a troop of boy scouts was offered for work on market gardens, again by Lady Catherine. Although that autumn pensioners were being approached to volunteer as labourers, a plan to identify market gardens willing to employ conscientious objectors from the Wakefield Work Centre failed when none could be found. January 1917 saw a survey of all available land in the area that could be used for crops or allotments and by May, 1,000 soldiers had been released to work around Wakefield alongside the Women's Land Service Corps. A year later, 2,110 men of the Agricultural Battalion at York had been sent to help. The shortage of horses was slowly being made up for by the introduction of motor tractors from 1917, but it would still be a close run race as to whether the Germans would be defeated before Britain starved.

Ever growing casualty lists, long and dangerous hours at work, food shortages and the threat of bombing all meant that raising a family was more challenging than ever. Shortly after the opening day of the Battle of the Somme, Westgate Chapel magazine reported on its Sunday School feast day in a field provided by Mr Swallow and with catering by Charles Hagenbach. 'The younger scholars happily do not realise the significance of war sufficiently to allow the thought of it to spoil their pleasure in the feast day but the seniors, the teachers and the parents could not but think of the young men who but for the war would have been present at the feast and especially of those who had taken or were then taking part in the great battle on the Somme and about whom news was anxiously awaited.'

Against such a background, wives and mothers attempted to keep the family together. Over £2 million per week was paid via the Post Office to just under 3 million dependants of men fighting overseas, but the allowances were small and rarely enough to keep pace with rising costs. One small, but very significant rise came in June 1918. In 1913, a rural town might expect up to twelve postal deliveries a day but by 1918 there would be only one as deliveries by road were reduced to conserve fuel and Travelling Post Offices (trains that conveyed mail) had their timetables adjusted to accommodate these service reductions. The Treasury had been drained by the huge costs of the war and the government needed to raise extra revenue by all possible means. The standard national postage rate of one penny for letters had stood for seventy years but it, too, fell victim to the war when the price was raised by a half penny.

As the war drew to a close, a final and even more deadly menace surfaced. In October 1918 reports were coming in of an increasing number of cases of a new strain of influenza. There had been sporadic outbreaks throughout the war, including one in March, but this was different. In the United States, army doctor Dr Roy Grist was working at Camp Devens near Boston: 'These men start with what appears to be an ordinary attack of la grippe or influenza, and when brought to the hospital they very rapidly develop the most vicious type of pneumonia that has ever been seen. Two hours after admission they have the mahogany spots over the cheekbones, and a few hours later you can begin to see cyanosis extending from their ears and spreading all over the face, until it is hard to distinguish the coloured men from the white ... It is only a matter of a few hours then until death comes ... It is horrible. One can stand it to see one, two, or twenty men die, but to see these poor devils dropping like flies ... We have been averaging a hundred deaths per day ... It takes special trains to carry away the dead. For several days there were no coffins.'

Widely known as Spanish Flu because neutral Spain had no press censorship and could report freely on the worldwide epidemic, the symptoms shown by its victims soon gained it a new nickname – 'the blue death'. It struck with such devastating speed that someone symptom-free at breakfast could be dead by evening and unlike other strains, this flu appeared to strike healthy young people aged 20–30 more than the young or old and, it seemed, those who should have had the strongest immune systems were, unexpectedly, the most vulnerable. Troops in the front lines came to regard being hospitalised as a virtual death sentence. As one survivor later recalled, 'It didn't last long – it would either kill you, or just go. The ones that went into hospital, we were hearing the day afterwards that they'd died. It would kill you in 24 hours – two days at most. That's when men started refusing to go into hospital. I know we lost more men from flu, day for day, than we did during the war.'

At home, special measures were put in place. In many areas schools closed completely for weeks at a time and restrictions were put on children attending cinemas, churches and shops, which all emptied as people sought to avoid contact with potential carriers. Newspapers were filled with adverts like those for Veno's Lightning Cough Cure promising 'instantaneous relief' or preventatives like Jeyes Fluid which was recommended for spraying 'the atmosphere of the office, factory, home and cinema ... disinfect lavatories, sinks and drains'. The *News of the World* advised readers to 'wash inside the nose with soap and water each night and morning: force yourself to sneeze night and morning, then breathe deeply; do not wear a muffler; take sharp walks regularly and walk home from work; do not "dope"; eat plenty of porridge'. None of which helped. The *Yorkshire Evening Post* was more practical: 'Do not ignore a feverish cold, no matter how slight the symptoms may be ... Go to bed and remain there until the symptoms abate. Keep entirely apart from children and old people ... use your common sense under all circumstances, and think of others'.

Figures for flu deaths in Wakefield were not published but every week the paper contained stories of local people who had fallen victim. Some measure of the scale of the disaster comes from Sheffield where the week up to 4 November had seen 468 people die – more in a single week than the Sheffield Pals battalion lost in the entire war. In neighbouring Leeds, 409 people died that week, 202 directly of influenza with 207 flu-related cases of complications like pneumonia. The death rate, it was reported, stood at 51.2 per thousand instead of the normal 15 or 16. Men came home from years of war to find their families wiped out by disease at home.

Worn out after four years of deprivation, illness, fear and stress, the people of Wakefield could celebrate the end of the war in 1918 but would take generations to come to terms with what had happened in those momentous years. The Defence of the Realm Act had reached into every aspect of daily life and the war had touched every man, woman and child in the country. It is a time remembered for seeing the death of a generation but the national tragedy owed as much to germs as to Germans. In six months Britain lost an estimated 200,000 civilians at a rate double that of the worldwide war. Today, the impact of Spanish Flu has largely been forgotten but the shock of the epidemic would be felt for years to come. At home, rationing had actually improved the diet of the poor. Women had found a strength, ability and independence unthinkable just a few years earlier. Sometimes for the worse, often for the better, the war had changed everything.

CHAPTER 9

Armistice and After

In 1917, the infamous Passchendaele Offensive had been launched to try to dislodge the German navy from Belgian ports and relieve the threat to merchant ships bringing supplies to Britain. At the time, the government had reckoned that the country would be facing starvation within months. As 1918 dawned, rationing was widespread and compulsory 'meat free' days had been introduced every week. One note of optimism came from America's entry into the war and it was this that prompted Germany to launch one last, desperate gamble to break the Allies before they could be reinforced. At 4.40am on 21 March, 6,000 German guns, supported by 3,500 trench mortars, rained 1,160,000 shells onto the British trenches as specially trained 'Stormtroopers' crept through thick fog and smoke to infiltrate the lines and pave the way for an attack by sixty-six divisions of infantry. The sudden attack was devastating on the depleted British front line as it tried to adjust to a reorganisation forced on it by the government in order to avoid having to send out more troops, despite the thousands of trained men currently being held in Britain. With so many shortages, troops were needed to shore up agriculture and industry at home and that, for the moment, took priority.

Private Arthur Pearson, of the Leeds Pals, later recalled the sense of urgency as news broke of the German attack: 'In the middle of the night, we runners were turned out as urgent messages had to be delivered to recall outlying detachments. Jerry had broken through our lines and was rapidly sweeping all before him. I was detailed to contact our boxing team and lead them to a point where the whole battalion was to be picked up by buses and rushed to the line. We got into "battle order", piled our packs in a field (we never saw them again, or our personal effects) and followed our guide across country to a line of old trenches which were held by the remnants of a battalion who had been badly cut up and had been retiring for days. We took over from them, stayed that night in those trenches, then, in daylight, began to retire.' His colleague Percy Barlow remembered: 'We arrived, after a 12-hour ride, at a lonely spot on the shell scarred road, from which we could see several villages on fire, the ruddy glow lighting the blackness for miles. Here, after dumping all unnecessaries, we were collected together ... and then we were quietly told that our task was to hold a trench one foot deep and to hold it at all costs.'

Lieutenant Cecil Slack of the East Yorkshire Regiment wrote home to say, 'The whole "show" has been absolute Hell. Several times we have been surrounded, and yet have managed to get away. There have been times when we have been almost touching the Boche – he with vastly superior numbers – and it has been a case of giving ourselves up or running for it, and we have run for it, and some of us live to fight another day. I felt an awful coward the first time I ran, but the only alternative was to become a prisoner. Once I was shot at by a party of Boches at under 50 yards range ... The nights have been very cold, and sleep an unheard of thing, just an odd hour here and there ... I cannot as I said before tell you all, what I have written only gives a tiny fraction of what has happened, I thank God I am alive to tell it.' For a time, it looked as if the Germans might actually be able to destroy the Allied armies. In a Special Order of the Day on 11 April, the Commander of the British Expeditionary Force, General Haig, made no attempt to conceal the danger: 'There is no other course open to us but to fight it out, every position must be held to the last man. There must be no retirement; with our backs to the wall and believing in the justice of our cause each of us must fight on to the end. The safety of our homes and the freedom of mankind alike depend upon the conduct of each one of us at this critical moment.'

Fortunately for the British, the German army was suffering the impact of years of blockade by the Royal Navy and the attacking Germans lost momentum as troops looted British supply dumps for food and equipment. Two days after Haig's message, the War Diary of 1/4 KOYLI noted that the battalion had captured seventeen Germans in the nearby YMCA canteen. By the end of the month, the offensive had ended. For 1/4 KOYLI, it had cost around 140 men dead from all causes and over 300 wounded. Caught in heavy fighting around Bucquouy, near Arras, 2/4 KOYLI lost fifty-two killed, eighty wounded and 268 missing, between 27 and 31 March alone. Along the lines, thousands of British troops were captured by the advancing Germans. In the wake of the March Offensive, Private George Ainley, of Sheffield, became the only KOYLI Territorial to be executed for desertion. Ainley served with 1/4 KOYLI and in January had been court-martialled for causing a self-inflicted wound. In July he was again tried, this time for two counts of desertion and one of being absent without leave. At the time, a charge of desertion meant that the accused had not intended to return to his unit, absent without leave meant he had not been with the unit but there was no evidence he intended to never return and despite popular belief, very few men were actually executed for 'cowardice' – a separate military crime. The facts were that 20-year-old Ainley had deserted twice and made two other attempts to avoid service in the same conditions as the rest of the battalion. It is easy from a twenty-first century perspective to claim he was the victim of post-traumatic stress and of an uncaring and barbarous military system, but every soldier arriving in France was made fully aware of the consequences of desertion. Ainley attempted to avoid serving in the front line, the rest of his unit didn't. As a result, they would have to work harder and take greater risks to make up for his absence. It is worth noting that he wasn't tried after his first attempt or even his second, when the risk of being shot would no doubt have been explained to him in no uncertain terms and he was reported as 'altogether lacking a sense of responsibility and his military character in consequence is not good.' For the military authorities, there were few options. A prison sentence would encourage desertion if the only punishment was to be the safety of a prison cell far behind the lines. At the same time, over 90 per cent of death penalties were not carried out and of those that were, some were on men who had previously been through the court martial system, been sentenced to death, shown leniency and yet had then done it again. There was often little sympathy among soldiers for those who deserted: 'If you desert,' one said, 'and let your friends down and left them to do your fighting for you, you deserved what you got.' Whether Ainley truly deserved his fate is open to debate but, along with the others who were found guilty of desertion, he was granted an official pardon in response to a political campaign in 2006.

To fill the gaps in the line, military regulations were changed. Previously, no-one could legally serve overseas until he reached the age of 19. It was agreed as a temporary measure that this could be reduced by six months, provided the soldier had at least six months of training behind him. In France, 2/4 KOYLI, now made up largely of teenage conscripts, hurriedly brought over to reinforce the losses of the

The manpower shortage became so severe that in 1918 the age for overseas service was reduced from 19 to 18½.

March Offensive, went into intensive training behind the lines and then were moved by train via Paris to the Champagne region, where German forces had reached the river Marne and were threatening Paris. In heavy fighting likened by some to jungle warfare, they recaptured the thick forests and open fields as the trench stalemate finally began to break. Over late July and early August the Germans were pushed back from the Marne and all along the Western Front the British pressed home attack after attack, beating back the enemy in a series of spectacular victories until finally, the Germans sued for peace. An Armistice came into force at 11.00am on 11 November 1918. At precisely that time, the guns fell silent. In one sector held by the KOYLI, a German machine gun fired one last burst before its crew stood, saluted the men they had been firing at and then turned their backs and slowly walked away.

Major S.G. Beaumont, of 2/4 KOYLI wrote to his wife: 'Sweetheart – well it has come at last. The day we have always longed for, for four weary years. I got it over the 'phone today at 9.15am from

Brigade. It's surprising how we all took it. Practically no excitement – I suppose really our feelings are too deep. We are carrying on just as usual. I've been writing my history of the last battle. I suppose really it's a greater relief to you than me. I ought to be, and am, very thankful I've come through.' Elsewhere, Major Lancelot Spicer, serving in 9 KOYLI, noted:

Armistice Day, November 11 1918
South of Maubeuge
Troops marching along the roads by platoons at intervals – a fresh autumn day. An early telegram has given the expected news 'operations will cease at 11a.m.' The men cannot grasp it – they have become so used to this soldier life, so numbed to endurance that they find it hard to believe they can live otherwise. At 11 o'clock, under orders (and for that reason only!) the troops are halted and give three cheers – but there is no enthusiasm. Of course they are glad it is all over – but they do not realise it. And that was the end of the greatest war that history has ever known.

In many cases, the end of the war seemed almost an anticlimax. Those who were teenagers or in their early twenties had been soldiers for their whole adult life. There were strong calls from ordinary soldiers for the advance to continue into Germany itself, that British troops should march through Berlin. With British industry and its workforce almost exhausted and the economy virtually bankrupted by war loans, that would never happen. The only men to march through Berlin's streets were German, and soon a myth began to grow that the German army had not been defeated, it had been stabbed in the back by weak politicians and their Jewish paymasters. A twice decorated former corporal in the 16th Bavarian Reserve Regiment eagerly adopted the view and began his rise to power. Hitler had seen his company reduced from 250 to sixty-two men in the first few months of the war and had served throughout, lying wounded in a hospital bed when the end came. 'When I was confined to bed, the idea came to me that I would liberate Germany, that I would make it great. I knew immediately that it would be realized.' For now, though, Germany lay humiliated.

In the wake of an influenza outbreak earlier in the year, Dr Hartley, medical superintendent of the Normanton and District Joint Isolation Hospital, had told the committee that quinine and cinnamon had both been put forward as a cure but in his opinion, a ban on the 'pernicious habit of kissing would be more efficacious. Probably the unnecessary amount of kissing prevalent today might be attributed to a flood of sentiment let loose by the war. In urgent cases, where total abolition would be a hardship, a small book of kissing coupons could be allowed provided that proper antiseptic precautions were taken.' As another, far more deadly outbreak swept the nation, all children were banned from any place of entertainment for two weeks in an attempt to limit contact with others, but news of the Armistice far outweighed people's fears and celebratory kisses were showered on servicemen as news reached home that the war was finally over.

Early on 11 November, news that the Germans had agreed a cease-fire at 5.00am to come into force at 11.00 began to circulate and as the hour approached, crowds began to gather outside the post office and those of the local newspaper, eager for the first confirmation that the war was truly over. 'At Wakefield, the Town Hall bell was rung, and later the residents heard with delight the Cathedral peal. The streets were quickly thronged with people. Practically all the works and places of business closed at noon and the school children were given a half-holiday. All the streets were decked with flags and streamers'. In the afternoon, 'citizens gathered in force in front of the Town Hall where a short Thanksgiving service was held ... The Mayor (Mr E. Blakey) said this was the greatest day that England ever knew – the day we had been looking forward to throughout all those black years. They were there that day to thank God they did not hoist the white flag. (Cheers). Britain and the Allies had been fighting for justice and for honourable peace and, above all, for freedom'.

For every man, woman and child, there was a pause as the enormity of the news sank in. For four years, the war had been at the centre of everyday life. Everything had revolved around it from the meagre breakfast rationing allowed to the long hours worked to keep the front supplied to the after work trip to the pub. DORA had governed so much of life but if the country was no longer under attack, was the Defence of the Realm Act still needed? The situation was perhaps best summed up by an officer who described his men's reaction: 'The quiet manner in which the troops received the news of an Armistice was remarkable,' he said. 'Their attitude, their conversation, all expressed the question, "And what happens now?"'

It was a reasonable question. Within weeks, men in the forces and their families at home were becoming restless. They had signed on for the 'duration of war' and now it was over, they wanted to get on with their lives. Protests and 'soldier strikes' broke out in camps across England and France over the delay in releasing men back to civilian life. The Russian Revolution had created an atmosphere of fear across Europe and the British government were no exception. British troops were already deployed in Russia as part of an international force sent to help fight the Bolsheviks in an attempt to prevent the spread of communism to other countries but fears were growing of some sort of revolution in Britain. The Volunteer Training Corps, formed as an amateur Home Guard, had developed into a well trained and reliable force. The threat of invasion was gone but the force was not stood down, kept on hand in case of serious disturbances at home by Socialists inspired by the Russian example. Strikes across the country involved workers and even the police and a protest march of thousands of soldiers was stopped outside London by other soldiers armed with rifles and bayonets.

The survivors of Wakefield's Territorials marched across the German border at Christmas 1918. It was to be a limited occupation along the Rhine partly to demonstrate victory and partly to act as a buffer in case peace talks broke down. Orders issued to the KOYLI warned that 'if peace negotiations fail, notice of the termination of the Armistice in 72 hours will be given to the Germans. The day on which the Armistice ceases will be called "J" Day.' In other words, the war could resume at any moment. At the same time, over 8 million men had served in the forces in the previous four years and getting them back into civilian life could not be accomplished overnight. Many had left their jobs to enlist and would be unemployed when they got home. Priority had to go to those who could administer the system, those who had jobs to go back to and those who would be of more value at home. Those who enlisted in 1914 thought they should be given priority regardless of their circumstances, those conscripted in 1918 argued they had been called up only for the period of hostilities. Attempting to calm the situation, the German-born Secretary of State For War, Lord Milner, explained that people should; 'Remember that, though the fighting may have ceased, all is not yet over. Impatience and over haste might yet rob us of all that four long years of unexampled struggle and sacrifice have won. We have yet to make a just, strong and enduring peace. When the representatives of Great Britain go to the Council table to negotiate that peace, they must not have a disarmed and disunited nation behind them. If we are all at sixes and sevens at home, if what remains of our Army is not compact, disciplined, orderly, we shall never get the sort of peace, which we justly expect. The world, which is still in many parts seething with disorder, may not settle down for years, or let us get back to normal life and work in safety and tranquillity ... Our guiding principle was to demobilise in the way most likely to lead to the steady resumption of industry, and to minimise the danger of unemployment. Pivotal men first, basic industries like coal mining before those of less vital importance. In each industry those men first, who were assured of immediate employment. Subject to these ruling principles, we want to release the older men, and those of longest service, before the younger ones. That is the general idea. I don't say that it can ever be perfectly executed. Certainly the execution isn't perfect yet. When the huge engine began to move, some defects immediately appeared in the machinery. These are being remedied. Some officials may have been stupid or obstructive. I am afraid, where thousands of people have to co-operate, there will always be a good sprinkling of muddlers. But when all is said and done the big engine is moving. It is moving at a steadily increasing pace.'

Wakefield Territorials were among the few British troops to enter Germany in 1918 as a deterrent in case peace talks broke down.

Slowly, things began to return to some sort of normality. The Food Control Committee remained in operation, but the good news was that tea had been removed from the ration in December. Supplies began to get back to normal and men started to come home. But that brought its own problems: they needed jobs but the end of the war meant an end to munitions work and it would take time for peace-time production to resume. War workers were being laid off with a promise of a few weeks' pay to tide them over and those jobs still available were often being done by women. Former munitionette Helen Bagnall of Castleford wrote to the papers to complain that one of her colleagues had told her: 'I am ashamed to let it be known that I have worked at Barnbow because wherever we go in the town we are jeered at, sneered at and insulted by men because they say we have no right to the Government's promise of 3s-9d a day for a few weeks or until we can find employment.' Surely, she argued, the men would not begrudge them thirteen weeks of pay until they could find work elsewhere.

Then on 28 June, exactly five years after that fateful shot was fired in Sarajevo, a peace treaty was signed at Versailles. The war was over. Unlike the Armistice, the celebrations that followed were organised and lavish. 'The Peace celebrations at Wakefield,' reported the *Yorkshire Evening Post*, 'are to extend from the 12th to the 19th inst. The streets in the vicinity of the Town Hall are to be decorated and also the route of the procession to the park. Bands will play in various parts of the city during Saturday morning and all places of business will be closed for the day... In Clarence Park a gala is to be held, and also a baby show. On the following Tuesday the school children will be given tea at their schools and will afterwards attend sports. Three thousand demobilized men are to be entertained to dinner in batches of 600 nightly on the five nights during Peace Week and a smoking concert is to follow.' Trams were to run as usual but workers would get double pay and a day in lieu. A tree was to be planted in commemoration of the event and a special medal was awarded by the City to all its returned men who had endured imprisonment in Germany as Prisoners of War. Local MP Colonel Sir E.A. Brotherton presented 8,000 local children with a bank book, each containing a deposit of a shilling to start their savings.

Amongst the frivolity, there were serious issues to be addressed. Wakefield were due to play cricket against Cleckheaton in the Heavy Woollen District Challenge Cup and wanted to field the son of the

Bishop of Wakefield, who had recently joined the club. He had played cricket at public school before the war but had joined the forces at the start of the war, now almost five years earlier, at the age of 16. He had been discharged only a few days before the committee met. The problem was whether he should be eligible to play. The rules said no and the committee would not budge until a compromise was reached; Wakefield would have to ask Cleckheaton if they were willing to let him play.

For a week, the joy of having survived the past few years surfaced but as the *Knottingley Express* put it: '... beneath the gaiety of the crowd there was the shadow of the absence of the departed, and it was to be noted as the procession passed that there were glistening eyes of mother, widow, sister, or sweetheart in window and doorway. It was, after all, a day of grief and remembrance for some.' Even as the Peace Week was still going on, the West Riding War Pension Committee met at Wakefield to discuss what would be a reasonable quota of disabled men in each type of workplace. Within a week of the celebrations, 250,000 miners across the country were on strike. Unusually, the strike had spread to the men who operated safety precautions to maintain the pits and the *Chicago Tribune* of 24 July reported that seven pits were already flooded, with a dozen more at serious risk if pumps were not started within 48 hours. The government response was to send in Royal Navy stokers to man the pumps and prevent flooding. Fearing reprisals, it also sent in armed troops to protect the sailors. They were not needed – even the most militant of the strikers knew that once a pit flooded it was lost and that attacking the sailors would mean the loss of their livelihoods so relations were generally good. It would set the pattern for the coming years. Britain had been almost bankrupted by fighting the war but its people had fought in the belief of a better future. That future, it was hoped, included a better deal for all – the problem was how to deliver it.

In 1920, a town meeting heard suggestions for how to honour the war dead. Plans were put forward for a new bridge over the Calder, a museum and art gallery, homes for disabled soldiers, the restoration of the Chantry, the purchase of old buildings and their restoration, a civic building, a club, a nurse's home. Everyone, it seemed, had a different idea and not all seemed to be putting commemoration of the war first. In the end, on Sunday, 13 November 1921, Alderman Blakey and members of the Corporation attended a service at Wakefield Cathedral in memory of all who had fallen in the war. It was followed

Wakefield's War Memorial.

by the unveiling of Wakefield's own cenotaph in the grounds of Clayton Hospital. It soon lay bedecked in flowers and wreaths. As the nation began to look ahead, there were still 122 soldier patients held in the Pauper Asylum at Wakefield, their only reward for their service the 2s-6d a week for special comforts and a promise that they would not end up in a pauper's grave.

The men, women and children who survived those tumultuous years are almost all gone. Soon, no child will ever again have chance to speak to someone who was alive when the events of this book took place but hopefully, from time to time, someone will look at Wakefield's stark memorial and pause. The homes those men lived in, the pubs they drank in, the shops they visited and the parks they played in are all still here. Away from the traffic and the hustle and bustle of modern life, somewhere at the edge of hearing, the voices of a lost generation can still be heard by those willing to listen.

Select Bibliography

Anon, *German Prisoners in Great Britain* (Tillotson & Son, *c*.1916).

Clayton, D., *From Pontefract to Picardy* (Tempus, 2004).

Ministry of Munitions, *History of the Ministry of Munitions* (HMSO, 1922).

Johnson, M.K., *Saturday Soldiers* (Doncaster Museum Service, 2004).

Johnson, M.K., *Surely we are Winning?* (Propagator Press, 2007).

Magnus, L., *West Riding Territorials in the Great War* (Kegan Paul Trench Trubner & Co., 1920).

Pearce, C., *Comrades in Conscience* (Francis Boutle, 2001).

Scott, W.H., *Leeds in the Great War* (Leeds Libraries and Arts Committee, 1923).

Wyrall, E., *The History of the 62nd (West Riding) Division 1914–1919* (Bodley Head, 1928).

Newspapers:
Daily Mirror
Dewsbury Reporter
Huddersfield Daily Examiner
Huddersfield Weekly Examiner
Ossett Observer
Pontefract and Castleford Express
Wakefield Express
Yorkshire Post

Index